Aspects of the Tonal System of Kalaḅarị-Ịjọ

STANFORD MONOGRAPHS IN AFRICAN LANGUAGES

William R. Leben and Larry M. Hyman
Series Editors

The aim of the series is to disseminate information about as many African languages as possible, especially about ones that have been to some extent neglected in the past, and to focus on primary materials, such as word lists, paradigms, and grammatical sketches.

Aspects of the Tonal System of Kalaḅarị-Ịjọ

Otelemate Harry

CSLI PUBLICATIONS
Center for the Study of
Language and Information
Stanford, California

Center for the Study of Language and Information
Leland Stanford Junior University
Printed in the United States
08 07 06 05 04   1 2 3 4 5

Library of Congress Cataloging-in-Publication Data

Harry, Otelemate G.
Aspects of the tonal system of Kalabari-Ijo / by Otelemate G. Harry.

p. cm. – (Stanford monographs in African languages)

Includes bibliographical references.

ISBN 1-57586-482-7 (pbk. : alk. paper)

1. Kalabari dialect—Tone. I. Title. II. Series.

PL8276.95.K3H37   2004
496′.3–dc22   2004009476
CIP

∞ The acid-free paper used in this book meets the minimum requirements of the American National Standard for Information Sciences—Permanence of Paper for Printed Library Materials, ANSI Z39.48-1984.

Please visit our web site at
http://cslipublications.stanford.edu/
for comments on this and other titles, as well as for changes and corrections by the author and publisher.

Contents

Preface

This book presents, for the first time, a detailed descriptive account of aspects of the tonal system of Kalaḅarị-Ịjọ (hereafter Kalaḅarị), a lect of the Ijoid branch of the Niger-Congo phylum, spoken in the Niger-Delta area of Southern Nigeria. The aim is to provide further understanding of the interaction between segmental and tonal phonology on the one hand, and particularly of the complex interface between tonology and morphosyntax of Kalaḅarị. The account is presented within multi-tier approaches to tone.

Contrary to the more usual situation in Ịjọ and most West African languages, where tones associate from left to right, it will be shown that tone association proceeds from right to left in Kalaḅarị. Further, at the lexical and phrasal levels, vowel deletion will be shown to result in floating tones, which in the case of floating L tone, accounts for the occurrence of downstep.

Kalaḅarị being an Ịjọ lect has SOV word order, lexical items combine into syntactic phrases which are right-headed. At this level, the lexical tone and the morphological class of the initial item in the phrase will be seen to determine the melody of the phrase. The tonal head of the phrase can thus be seen to be the leftmost, whereas the syntactic head is rightmost in the phrase. The association of tones within the phrase proceeds from left to right, in accordance with the left-headness of the tone phrase.

The prosodic structure of the tone phrase can therefore be claimed to be built within the boundaries of the syntactic phrase, but independently of the syntactic structure within those boundaries. Finally, a difference in tonal behavior will be demonstrated which is based on the syntactic distinction between lexical and functional heads.

The study presented in this book is a revised version of my doctoral dissertation, awarded in May 1999. Most of the analysis in the previous version has been maintained in this version. However, I have revised crucial aspects of the analysis; for example, I have reorganized most of the data and revised the analysis of tonal patterns associated with loan words from English. In addition, I have extended the database with a list of lexical items in the Appendix.

This book would not have been possible without the support of persons and institutions in Nigeria, USA and the Caribbean. Space, time and memory constrain the mention of every individual who has contributed to the study contained in this book. My heart-felt gratitude goes to each one of them.

I owe special gratitude to Hubert Devonish, who whole-heartedly supported this project from its inception in 1995 and through to its completion in 2003. I am most grateful to Larry Hyman for his invaluable advice, comments and his infectious faith in this work and in my academic career. Many thanks to Will Leben who examined this work, as a doctoral dissertation in 1998, and saw its potential for publication. His active support eventually led to the successful publication of this version of the work. Sharon Inkelas deserves a special gratitude for serving as my host and facilitator during my three-month stay at the Department of Linguistics, University of California, Berkeley, in the summer of 1996. I owe a bundle of gratitude to the anonymous reviewer whose criticisms greatly improved the quality of this work.

I am grateful to Kay Williamson who steered me into Linguistics in 1983 at the University of Port Harcourt and has played a crucial role in my linguistics journey. In addition, I am grateful for her invaluable comments and suggestions for improvement of this work. Many thanks to my former colleagues in the Department of Linguistics and African Languages, University of Port Harcourt, Charles E.W. Jenewari, Shirley Donwa-Ifode, Emmanuel Efere, Mrs. P. Ejele, Ozo-mekuri Ndimele and Jones Ayuwo, for their moral and academic support.

I would like to thank the following colleagues at the Mona and St. Augustine campuses of the University of the West Indies, for their unstinting support at various stages of the research for this work: Mervyn Alleyne, Kathryn Brodber, Joe Pereira, Silvia Kouwenberg, Alison Irvine, Danis Jaganaugth, Ian Robertson, Selteca, Mitchell Ennis and Yvette Mundy-White.

My sincere gratitude goes to all members of my family for their overwhelming support, especially Mother, Love, my sisters; Dasoba and Idaeresoari, and my brothers; Truman, Endwell, Amieyeofori, and Sobomabo. Thanks to Imade and my children, Otelemate and Tonye, for their understanding. Many thanks to Troy-Ann and Jade for their love. Also, thanks to the publication team at CSLI Publications.

I gratefully acknowledge the University of the West Indies, Mona for funding my research trips to University of California at Berkeley and Stanford University in 1996, and in 1997, to the LSA Summer Institute at Cornell University, Ithaca and also contributing US$2,000.00 grant towards the publication of this work. Further, I would like to thank the Linguistic Society of America for the tuition fellowship award which enabled me to attend and participate in the activities of the 1997 Linguistic Institute held at Cornell University, Ithaca.

Any misrepresentations in terms of data, analysis and judgment in this work are entirely my responsibility.

Otelemate G. Harry
Department of Language, Linguistics and Philosophy
University of the West Indies, Mona, Jamaica

1

Introduction

1.0 Preliminary Remarks

This chapter provides some information on the geographical location, and the linguistic classification of Kalaḅarị.[1] Furthermore, an overview of the segmental and syllable phonology and the syntactic structures will be presented. Aspects of these will inform our discussion of tone in the chapters to follow.

1.1 The Speakers and Their Location

Kalaḅarị is spoken in three Local Government Areas of Rivers State, Nigeria, namely; Degema, Ásárị-tọ́rū̩ and Ákụ́kụ́- tọ́rū̩. These areas are situated in the Eastern Niger-Delta Area of the State. The people call themselves and are known by their neighbors as Kalaḅarị, but sometimes their Igbo neighbors call them **ḿba ḿmīrí**[2] 'water people', because the Kalaḅarị people live in the Niger-Delta area of South-Eastern Nigeria. The Kalaḅarịs have traditionally, pursued fishing and trading as their primary economic activities. With Western education and other avenues for self-advancement, people have generally drifted to places (local and overseas) other than their Kalaḅarị settlements and acquired other skills that would realize their life's ambitions.

[1] In the orthographic representations of names of towns and villages acute accent marks high tone, macron (-) marks downstepped high tone, while low tone is left unmarked. Further, vowels with subdots indicate [-ATR] and subdots on b and d indicate implosives.

[2] Dike (1956: 30) records 'ndi mili nnu (people of the salt water)' as an earlier expression used by their Igbo neighbors.

The Kalaḅarị linguistic area spreads over three major islands and twenty-five other smaller islands.[3] These communities constitute the New-Calabar City-State in the Niger Delta until the nineteenth and early twentieth centuries. The New Calabar City State in the Niger Delta is a pre-colonial formation (Warịḅọkọ 1991: 42-109).

The three major Kalaḅarị islands are Buguma (Ásárị́), Abonnema (Nyémọ́nị́) and Bakána. The rest are Tómbía, Abalama, Áḅị́ssa, Angụlamáa, Ḅákána, Ḅíllé, Ịdọ, Ị́fọ́kọ, Íléléma, Ke, Krákráma, Kụ́lá, Mịnamáa, Ọḅụama, Ọkpọ́ọ, Óproamáa, Órú-káláma, Sangamáa, Órú-sángáma, Sokúu, Tẹ́ma, Omékwéáma, Ọ́bōnọ́ma,[4] Sẹmáa and Ékulamáa.

The Kalaḅarị people migrated to these islands from earlier settlements that are now more of historical sites, although small communities of Kalaḅarị speakers can still be found in the older settlements (Warịḅọkọ 1991: 50-109).

Although rivers and creeks separate these islands, Kalaḅarị is fairly homogenous (Jenewari 1977, Harry 1989). However, very recent surveys, for example, Harry (in progress) have shown that innovations are emerging in some of the islands. Ḅíllé has developed a tonal system that is noticeably different from the rest. Tómbía also has slight tonal differences. However, these differences do not impede intelligibility between Ḅíllé and Tómbía speakers on one hand and the rest of the speakers in the other islands on the other hand.

Wolff (1959) and Jenewari (1977, 1984) report the use of Kalaḅarị[5] as a second language outside of the immediate geographical and administrative units described above. These communities are Kụgbọ́ọ, Ọdual, Abúan, Ẹngẹ́nnị, and some Ikwérré communities such as Ẹ́mọ́hụa and Ọgbakịrị (all in Rivers State).

It has also been reported by Jenewari (1984, 1989) that the Kalaḅarịs were among the first West Africans to come in contact with the European traders/colonizers. One of the consequences of Kalaḅarị contact with Dutch European merchants is that the Kalaḅarị including their Eastern Ịjọ relatives (Okrika and Ịḅanị) were transported (during the slave trade) to Berbice colony, what is now, in Guyana.

As reported by Smith et. al. (1987) and Kouwenberg (1993: 119, 1996: 343-344), Kalaḅarị (Eastern Ịjọ) contributed significantly to the formation of Berbice Dutch Creole.

[3]Within the Kalaḅarị speech community there are two non-Ịjọ speech communities, namely Degema and Ḅúkúma, who are within the administrative unit of Degema Local Government Authority. The speakers of Degema (Delta-Edoid) and Ḅúkúma (Central Delta language) are bilingual in their respective languages and Kalaḅarị.

[4]Ọ́bọ̄nọ́ma was originally a Delta-Edo speech community. The language is 'virtually extinct' (Elugbe 1989: 294). The same applies to Ịdọ, who originally spoke Delta-Cross language (now extinct).

[5]The use of Kalaḅarị in these communities is as a result of the central role the Kalaḅarịs played in commercial activities in the Niger Delta between late eighteenth and early nineteenth centuries (Wariboko 1998: 110-189).

1.2 Kalaḅarị in Ịjọ Classification

Kalaḅarị is one of the four lects of KOIN (Eastern Ịjọ), a sub-branch of the Ịjọ language cluster. The others are Okrika, Ịḅanị and Nkọrọ́ọ. Okrika and Ịḅanị are more mutually intelligible to Kalaḅarị, while Nkọrọ́ọ is less so (Harry 2003: 113). KOIN plus three other sub-branches, Nembe-Akassa (Akaha), Ịzọn and Inland Ịjọ constitute the Ịjọ language cluster in the Niger-Congo Phylum.

Williamson and Blench (2002: 22) split Ịjọ into two major branches; East and West. East is divided into Nembe-Akassa (Akaha) and KOIN. The West is split into Inland Ịjọ and Ịzọn. This internal sub-grouping, however, differs from Jenewari (1989) proposal. However we will not go into any details of the differences and similarities of the two classifications since it is not crucial to this study.

Ịjọ combines with Defaka to constitute the Ijoid sub-group of Atlantic-Congo in the Niger-Congo phylum. Defaka is the closest linguistic relative of Ịjọ, (Jenewari 1983).[6]

1.3 Kalaḅarị Literature

Research on Kalaḅarị has been quite limited, particularly so in relation to the tone system. Discussion here will cover the available descriptive data and technical theoretical analyses of the Kalaḅarị tone system. The earliest records of Kalaḅarị are given my European travelers and missionaries. Jenewari (1984: 10, 1989: 105) reports the first recorded data were the numerals, one to five by Olfert Dapper, a Dutch traveler, in 1668. Word lists are also found in Clarke (1848) and Thomas (1914).

Two native speakers of Kalaḅarị produced primers in the lect. Harry (1949) wrote **Kalaḅarị Tarị Go Ḍiri** 'Kalaḅarị First Reader'. Akoḅo (1953) wrote **Wa Nimi n'iḅi Aị** 'Things We Ought to Know'. The Government of Rivers State also sponsored the production of literature in the native languages for use by primary school pupils in the state. For Kalaḅarị, this resulted in the production of a primer by Berepiki (1971) entitled **Kalaḅarị Tarị Go Ḍiri**. Williamson (1972) wrote **Reading and Writing Kalaḅarị**. Jenewari (1972) wrote Teachers' Note on **Kalaḅarị Tarị Go Ḍiri** and in 1974 wrote **Kalaḅarị Orthography** (second edition in 1978).

More serious linguistic descriptions of Kalaḅarị are given in Wolff (1959) and Ladefoged (1964). Both provide brief phonological sketches of the lect. Undergraduate students at the University of Port Harcourt have written long essays describing various aspects of the phonology of Kalaḅarị, for example, Iḅim (1983) on **The Phonology of Ḅíllé**, Iyalla (1984) on **A Comparative Analysis of Suprasegmentals in Ḅụmọ and Kalaḅarị** and Dateme (1985) on **Contrastive Analysis of the Phonology of Kalaḅarị and Kiswahili**. These undergraduate essays have as their reference point the phonological description of Kalaḅarị given in Jenewari (1977).

[6] Williamson and Blench (2000: 22) provide the internal classification of Ijoid.

A detailed descriptive and theoretical account of Kalaḅarị syntax based on the syntactic theory developed in Chomsky (1965) and in his subsequent work, is given in Jenewari's doctoral dissertaion, **Studies in Kalaḅarị Syntax** (1977). In this study, an attempt was also made to provide a description of Kalaḅarị tonal system. Jenewari (1977: 91) states that Kalaḅarị has two lexical tones, High and Low, with a phonemic downstep. Words show a number of combinational possibilities with these tones. Furthermore, he gives some descriptive data that show tone change in certain phrasal constructions. These phrase types are summarized in (1) below (Jenewari 1977: 95-99).

(1) Tone Change in Phrase Types
Words in a simple Noun Phrase
Object-NP + V in a simple Verb Phrase

Jenewari observes that, most frequently, the initial word retains its tone melody, while the tone of the word in non-initial position is reduced. In the tonal sketch given there, he does not attempt to provide any theoretical account of tone processes in the lexical and phrasal components of the phonology, the focus of his study being the syntactic structures of the lect. Nevertheless his work does indicate awareness that the complex nature of morphotonemic processes is an area of Kalaḅarị phonology that needs further investigation.

Williamson (1988) provides a tonal account of Kalaḅarị within a comparative analysis of Ịjọ pitch systems. Williamson gives an analysis of Ịjọ pitch systems within the version of Lexical Phonology proposed by Pullyblank (1986). Besides Kalaḅarị, she considered three other Ịjọ lects, namely, Kolokuma, Nembe and Ḅụmọ. The consequences of her analysis are considered in Chapter 5 of this study.

Akinlabi (1955, 1997) has proposed a very insightful analysis of Kalaḅarị vowel harmony system within the prevailing framework of Optimality Theory (OT). Some aspects of his analysis are incorporated in sections of this Chapter. The list of works given here is by no means exhaustive, but is crucial to the present study. Mostly recently, Harry (2003) provides an illustration the IPA within Kalaḅarị phonology.

1.4 Kalaḅarị Segmental Phonology

Presented here are aspects of the phonology and syntactic structures of Kalaḅarị. The focus is on those structures relevant to the behavior of tone. From now on data are presented in phonemic transcriptions, using the IPA where necessary. Other symbols will be explained when encountered.

1.4.1 Vowel System

Eighteen phonetic vowels occur in Kalaḅarị. The features of Height, [high] and [low], [back] and [nasal] determine these vowels. In addition, Advanced Tongue Root, henceforth [ATR], plays a significant role in distinguishing vowels in Kalaḅarị. I illustrate the eighteen vowels in Figure 1.1 below.

	+ATR				-ATR			
	-back		+back		-back		+back	
	- Nasal	+ Nasal	- Nasal	+ Nasal	- Nasal	+ Nasal	- Nasal	+ Nasal
+h	i	ĩ	u	ũ	ɪ	ɪ̃	ʊ	ʊ̃
-h	e	ẽ	o	õ	ɛ	ɛ̃	ɔ	ɔ̃
+l.							a	ã

Figure 1.1: Phonetic Vowel Inventory of Kalaḅarị

From Figure 1.1, it is obvious that every oral vowel has a nasal counterpart. It is also clear that every [+ATR] vowel has a [-ATR] counterpart except for [a] and [ã], which do not have corresponding [+ATR] counterparts.

The occurrence of nasality in vowels is unpredictable. However, as demonstrated in Akinlabi (1995), ATR is a morpheme feature and not part of the underlying representation of the vowel. Given that ATR is a morpheme feature, I follow Akinlabi by proposing that there are five oral and five nasal vowels constituting the underlying vowel inventory of Kalaḅarị. These are shown in Figure 1.2 below.

	Front		Back
High	i ĩ		u ũ
Mid	e ẽ		o õ
Low		a ã	

Figure 1.2: Phonemic Vowel Inventory of Kalaḅarị

Four features relevant to Kalaḅarị are selected from the repertoire of vowel features proposed by Halle and Clements (1983: 6-8). These features are [high], [back], [low] and [nasal]. Figure 1.3 provides a fully specified vowel matrix using the selected features.

	i	e	a	o	u	ĩ	ẽ	ã	õ	ũ
high	+	-	-	-	+	+	-	-	-	+
low	-	-	+	-	-	-	-	+	-	-
back	-	-	+	+	+	-	-	+	+	+
nasal	-	-	-	-	-	+	+	+	+	+

Figure 1.3: Vowel Feature Matrix of Kalaḅarị

The matrix in Figure 1.3 provides the features we will need to describe Kalaḅarị vowels in the morpheme structures and the formal phonological rules occurring throughout the study.

Notes on Vowels

All vowels occur in medial and final positions in the word, but a close back vowel never occurs in initial position if it is the only element in the syllable. Further investigation is needed on vowel distribution in morphemes in Kalaḅarị. Figure 1.4 gives a summary of vowel distribution in morpheme structure. '0' indicates onset, while the +, - signs indicate the presence or absence of a segment.

		i	e	a	o	u	ĩ	ẽ	ã	õ	ũ
Initial	+0	+	+	+	+	+	+	+	+	+	+
	-0	+	+	+	+	-	+	+	+	+	-
Medial	+0	+	+	+	+	+	+	+	+	+	+
	-0	+	+	+	+	+	+	+	+	+	+
Final	+0	+	+	+	+	+	+	+	+	+	+
	-0	+	+	+	+	+	+	+	+	+	+

Figure 1.4: Distribution of Vowels in Morphemes in Kalaḅarị

1.4.1.1 ATR Harmony

The [+ATR] is characterized by a relatively expanded pharynx, whereas [-ATR] is characterized by relatively reduced pharynx (Lindau 1978:550). Ladefoged & Maddieson (1996:300-304) present other articulatory features related to ATR. What is important, however, is that Kalaḅarị vowels harmonize in ATR-features. This prevents opposite values of ATR from occurring within a domain. However, [a], is the only [-ATR] vowel which can co-occur with vowels from either set. The vowels can be divided into two harmonic sets, as shown in (2) below.

	SET 1		SET 2	
(2)	[+ATR]		[-ATR]	
	i	u	ɪ	ʊ
	e	o	ɛ	ɔ
	(a)		a	

In Kalaḅarị, ATR occurs in two domains: intra-word and clitic domains. Please note that the term 'morpheme' as used in this study is synonymous with the term 'word'. The following data in (3) show the co-occurrence restrictions of vowels within a word domain.

(3)

a. Words with [+ATR]		b. Words with [-ATR]	
pìrǐ	'bush'	pìrɪ̀	'give'
kúꜜnú	'sour'	kʊ́ꜜnʊ́	'scent'
ɓélé	'distance'	ɓɛ́rɛ́	'case/trouble'
póꜜkó	'pull'	pɔ́ꜜkɔ́	'take by force'

c. [a] plus [+ATR] vowels		d. [a] plus [-ATR] Vowels	
àtí	'ten'	árʊ́	'canoe'
fúꜜrá	'be pregnant'	píꜜná	'white'
íɓílá	'bed'	dʊ̀ɓà	'large'

The data in (3) suggest that a word is specified for one ATR value only. ATR in this case is a word level feature in Kalaḅarị (Akinlabi 1995: 72-6, 1997). Words, not vowels, are specified for ATR.

Clitics

In the second domain, the harmony process occurs in clitics or possessive constructions in which possessive pronouns precede nouns; the pronoun is the possessor, while the noun is the possessed (Jenewari 1980: 90-91; Akinlabi 1995: 77, 1997: 6). The possessive forms,[7] as shown in (4), have two canonical variants, namely bi-/tri-syllabic ((C)V.CV(CV)) and monosyllabic (V). The bisyllabic variant precedes vowel-initial nouns, while a monosyllabic form precedes consonant-initial nouns.[8] For each bisyllabic and monosyllabic variant, there is the option to select its [-ATR] or a [+ATR] form depending on the ATR specification of the following noun.

(4)

a. Bi/tri-syllabic Clitic			b. Monosyllabic Clitic			
ìjè	~	ɪ̀jɛ̀	ì	~	ɪ̀	'me, my'
íjé	~	ɪ́jɛ́	í	~	ɪ́	'you(r) sg.'
òrǐ	~	ɔ̀rɪ̀	ò	~	ɔ̀	'he, his'
árǐ	~	árɪ̀	á			'her, hers'
ìnǐ	~	ɪ̀nɪ̀	ǹ			'they, their'
wá	~	wámɪ̀nɪ̀				'we, our'
		ɔ́mɪ̀nɪ̀	ó	~	ɔ́	'you(r) pl.'

This cross-boundary harmony between possessive pronouns and following nouns is exemplified in (5) and (6) below. Note that, in fast speech in this context and other regular phrasal constructions, the final vowel of the initial word completely assimilates to the initial onsetless vowel of the following morpheme. There is an optional process in which the two identical vowels contract into a single vowel. (Jenewari 1980: 15). The examples in (5) and (6) below illustrate.

[7]In the plural clitics, only the long ones can be used as possessive pronouns. In the possessive forms of these clitics, the last vowel [ɪ] is replaced by the plural suffix {-a} via vowel deletion.

[8]This constraint does not hold in plural clitic possessive constructions. Both V- and C-initial words follow the plural possessive forms.

(5) [+ATR] Constructions

a. Possessive pronouns followed by vowel-initial nouns

/ǐjè + òbìrì/ → [ǐjòòbí꜌rí] → [ǐjòbí꜌rí] 'my dog'
/ǐjè + íkù/ → [ǐjììkú꜌ú] → [ǐjìkú꜌ú] 'my cocoyam'
/íjé + òbìrì/ → [íjóóbí꜌rí] → [íjóbí꜌rí] 'your dog'

b. Possessive pronouns followed by consonant-initial nouns

/í + póló/ → [í pó꜌ló] 'your compound'
/á + ɓùrù/ → [á ɓú꜌rú] 'her yam'
/í + féní/ → [í fé꜌ní] 'your bird'

(6) [-ATR] Constructions

a. Possessive pronouns followed by vowel-initial nouns

/ǐjè + ɔ̀ɓɔ́꜌kɔ́/ → [ɪ̌jɔ̀ ɔ̀ɓɔ́꜌kɔ́] → [ɪ̌jɔ̀ɓɔ́꜌kɔ́] 'my fowl'
/íjé + ímbárá/ → [íjɔ́ ímbá꜌rá] → [íjímbá꜌rá] 'your sister'
/íjé + ɔ́ɓɔ́꜌kɔ́/ → [íjɔ́ ɔ́ɓɔ́꜌kɔ́] → [íjɔ́ɓɔ́꜌kɔ́] 'your fowl'

b. Possessive pronouns followed by consonant-initial nouns

/í + wá꜌rí/ → [í wá꜌rí] 'your house'
/á + ɓɛ́rɛ́/ → [á ɓɛ́꜌rɛ́] 'her trouble/problem'
/í + kápà/ → [í ká꜌pá] 'your dress'

1.4.1.2 Surface Vowel Deletion

Two domains of vowel deletion may be distinguished. These are vowel deletion word-internally and vowel deletion phrase-internally. Vowel deletion is triggered (i) at word level by a following nasal or (ii) at both word and phrase levels by a syllabic constraint that, except in very specific circumstances, prohibits V-V sequences in Kalaḅarị. In relation to (ii), I propose a surface syllabic structure constraint in (7) below.

(7) Surface Syllabic Structure Constraint (SSSC)
No vowels in sequence within a surface phonological domain.

a. Word Level * [...$V_1.V_2$...]
b. Phrase Level * [...V_1 # V_2...]$_{ph}$

Word-Level Vowel Deletion

A vowel deletion process occurs which involves the optional deletion of a word-initial high front vowel when it precedes a nasal in the coda. The nasal becomes syllabic as a result. The tone left by the deleted vowel is linked to the syllabic nasal, as shown in the examples in (8a) below.

(8) a. íŋ͡gbè → [ŋ́m͡gbè] 'oyster'
ìngàdá → [ŋ̀gàrá] 'seat'

b. ónbú → [ómbú] 'navel'
án꜌g͡bó → [áŋm꜌g͡bó] 'millipede'

Notice that the high front vowel is deleted in the forms in (8a), but that non-high vowels are not deleted in (8b).

Phrase-Internal Vowel Deletion

In an environment in which two vowels occur sequentially across a word boundary in the phrase, the vowel to the left is deleted. In fact, deletion follows assimilation, whereby the final vowel of the initial word assimilates to the initial onsetless vowel of the following word. However, the illustration in (9) below will not include the intermediate assimilatory process.

(9) a.	/ɪ̀nà + ɛ́rɛ́ɓɔ́/	→	[ɪ̀nɛ̀ rɛ́ɓɔ̀]	'their woman'
	/mȉndʒȉ + ópùró/	→	[mȉndʒò púrò]	'(a) water limpet'
	/pȉrȉ + íkù/	→	[pȉríkù]	'(a) bush cocoyam'
	/gógò + íkúlélè/	→	[gógȉ kùlélè]	'Gogo's(fem.) iron'
b.	/póló + ɔ̀ɓɔ́ꜜkɔ́/	→	[pólɔ́ ɓɔ́kɔ̀]	'(a)compound's fowl'
	/síɓɪ́ + àdáká/	→	[síɓá dákà]	'(a) head's rash'
	/wáꜜrí + èdʒȉmínà/	→	[wáꜜré dʒímínà]	'(a) house ram'

The forms in (9) show CV.V sequences occurring across a morpheme boundary in the underlying representations. It is clear that V deletion at phrasal level in Kalaḅarị is a distinct phenomenon from that which operates word internally.

Note that in the two domains vowel deletion generates surface CV sequences only, the preferred syllable structure in Kalaḅarị. However, the constraint does not apply to non-identical vowel sequences preceding a boundary at the word level. The data in (10) provide some examples of word final vowel sequences.

(10)	a.	pùá	'split'
	b.	sȉá	'separate'
	c.	fɔ̀ɪ	'roast'
	d.	pɛ̀ɪ	'eat (of fish or meat)'
	e.	sòàlá	'Name'

1.4.1.3 Sequentially Occurring Identical Vowels

Sequentially occurring identical vowels are found in four environments in the phonology. I list these environments in (11) below.

(11) Environments for identical vowels in Kalaḅarị
- a. Words in isolation with HLH tone melody.
- b. Phrase final words with HL tone melody.
- c. Verbs in the H Gerundive construction.
- d. Verbs in the HL imperative construction.

The data in (12) below illustrate these environments.

(12) a. Words in isolation with HLH

ɗúꜜú	'scoop'	tíꜜî	'play'
HLH		HLH	

b. Words in phrase final position with HL

òb̌ìřì + sòò → [òb̌ìřì sóò]		'(a) goat's destiny'
L L	L LL H L	
féní + sòò → [féní sóò]		'(a) bird's destiny'
HH L	H H HL	

c. Verbs in the Gerundive-H Construction

fìɪ H-Gerund	→ [fíɪ]	'dying'
L	L H	
tùù H-Gerund	→ [tùú]	'setting (trap)'
L	L H	

d. Verbs in the Imperative-HL Construction

tùù HL-Imperative	→ [tùúù]'set (trap)!'	
L	LHL	
sɔ̀ HL-Imperative	→ [sɔ̀ɔ́ɔ̀]	'cook!'
L	LHL	

To account for identical vowels in sequence in (12a) and (12b), I propose, following Leben (p.c.), that these words are underlyingly CV, but the V is lengthened in order to accommodate the following tone(s) in the melody. This proposal requires that surface monosyllabic words have a (C)V plus a segmentally unspecified V_2, representing an additional syllable that derives from the specified V. This V_2 on the surface takes on the features of the specified V with the additional tone in the melody, as the word has a two-tone melody. Thus, lengthening is arguably triggered by tone association. Similarly, V_3 in (12d) derives from V_1 via lengthening (details of tone melody are discussed in Chapter 2). Following this proposal, the examples in (13a) are well-formed, while those in (13b) are ill-formed on the surface.

(13) a.	sò L	'heaven/destiny'	b.	*sòò
	sá H	'debt'		*sáá

Previous explanation, given in the dissertation, is that words are minimally bisyllabic, /CV-V/. Thus, surface monosyllabic words have a CV plus a segmentally unspecified V-slot. Vowel deletion then explains (13a), but vowel deletion is blocked in words associated with multi-tonal melodies, as seen in the examples in (12). Of the two proposals, the former better captures facts presented in this study.

1.4.2 Consonant System

Twenty-two consonant phonemes occur in Kalaḅarị (Jenewari 1980: 7, Harry 2003: 113). An inventory of phonemic consonants of Kalaḅarị is listed in figure 1.5 below.

	Labial	Alveolar	Palatal	Velar	Labial-Velar	Glottal
Nasal	m	n				
Plosive	p b	t d	dʒ	k g	kp gb	
Implosive	ɓ	ɗ				
Trill		r				
Fricative	f v	s z				
Approximant		l	j		w	ɦ

Figure 1.5: Consonant Phoneme Inventory of Kalaḅarị

Note

Consonant distribution in syllables and word structures is simple and straightforward. Non-nasal consonants occur in syllable initial position only. Nasal consonants according to my analysis may occur both syllable-initially and syllable-finally. However, whereas syllable initially there is the phonemic distinction between /m/ and /n/, syllable finally it is /m/. This surfaces as [n], [ŋ], [ŋ͡m] or [m], homorganic with the following consonant which is always a stop, inclusive of affricates. Syllable-final nasals occur word-internally. In the underlying lexical specification of items, no syllable-final nasal occurs word-finally, except /m/ (Harry 2003: 115).

1.4.2.1 Implosive Harmony

Jenewari (1989: 109) reports that there is implosive harmony which occurs as a distributional constraint involving implosives /ɓ, ɗ/ and voiced anterior plosives /b, d/ in words. Thus, within such a word, members of the implosive set /ɓ, ɗ/ or members of the plosive set /b, d/ can co-occur, but implosives and plosives never co-occur. Velar stops however do occur with either set. The data in (14) illustrate the distribution of these consonant types.

(14) a.	Implosive		b.	Plosive	
	ɓíɓí	'mouth'		bébé	'whole'
	ɗáɓá	'dream'		bàdàrà	'very large'
	ɓʊ̀kɔ̀	'monkey'		búgúmà	'Búgúmà'
	ɗûgò	'tell'		dó↓kî	'carry'

Efere (1994: 19) also reports this type of harmony in Ḅụmọ, an Ịzọn lect of Ịjọ. In the feature system proposed in Halle and Clements (1983: 8) for consonants, implosives are distinguished from the plosives by the feature [constricted glottis], and this is the feature which will be used here to distinguish between the two kinds of consonants in Kalaḅarị.

1.4.2.2 Homorganic Nasal

The only consonantal process related to the discussion of tones in this study involves homorganic nasals. A homorganic nasal is a nasal in the coda that assimilates to the place of articulation of a following stop consonant. In autosegmental terms (cf. §2.3.2), the stop consonant spreads its place feature leftwards onto the preceding nasal. I give some examples of homorganic nasals in (15) below.

(15) a.	/ómbṹ/	→	[ómbṹ]	'navel'
b.	/kɔ̀mdʒù/	→	[kɔ̀ndʒù]	'waist'
c.	/ɪ̂mgʊ̀/	→	[ɪŋgʊ̀]	'frog'
d.	/ɪ́mkpáɾá/	→	[ɪ́ŋ͡mk͡páɾá]	'walking-stick'

It is these nasals, when preceded by an onsetless high vowel in word initial position, which can through the deletion of this vowel become syllabic and thus bear tone.

1.5 Syllable Structure and Types

The basic syllable structure in Kalaḅarị consists of an optional onset followed by a rhyme. The onset position is filled by a consonant, while the rhyme is filled by a nucleus (peak), which contains a vowel (V), and an optional coda, which is always a non-word final nasal. Thus the basic structure I assume in this study is given in (16) below. N occurs in non-final coda.

(16) Syllable Structure of Kalaḅarị
$(C^1_0)\ V^1_1\ (N^1_0\text{-})$

In (16) the superscript indicates the maximum, while the subscript indicates the minimum, number of segments allowed in the syllable. The structure in (16) shows that the vowel is the only obligatory element in the syllable. Kalaḅarị does not allow a coda other than a nasal in its rhyme. The syllable structure in (16) predicts four syllable types, as seen in (17) below. N represents a bilabial nasal in the coda.

(17) V, CV, CVN-, VN-

The first two of the four syllable patterns in (17), V and CV, can surface in any phonological environment. I therefore consider them basic syllable types in Kalaḅarị. The last two patterns, namely, CVN- and VN-, can only occur where there is a following (C)V syllable. I give some examples showing the four patterns in (18) below. Kalaḅarị has both oral and nasal vowels. Thus a syllable may either have an oral vowel or a nasal vowel.

(18) a.	sá	CV	'debt'	b.	sã́	CṼ	'urine'
c.	ɪ̂	V	'yes'	d.	ò	V	'he/his'
e.	kùmbù	CVN-CV	'axe'	f.	íŋgɔ́	VN-CV	'wealth'

It will be noted that, according to this analysis, [mb], [ŋg] etc. are not prenasalized stops. The reason is that these nasals become syllabic when a preceding vowel is deleted, as discussed in §1.4.2.2 above. I propose, instead, that they consist of a nasal in the coda of a preceding syllable and a stop consonant in the onset of the following syllable. Syllabification of the nasal portion of a prenasalized stop is not typical of prenasalized stops (Welmers 1973). There is, however, a weakness in this analysis. [N] occurs syllable-finally only, preceding a syllable with a stop consonant onset. It never occurs word-finally and is always homorganic with the following consonant. We may, therefore, be dealing with some kind of intermediate phenomenon. However, since this aspect of the analysis of Kalaḅarị syllable structure is not salient to tone, we will not pursue this issue any further here.

1.6 Aspects of Kalaḅarị Morphology and Syntax

The aspects of the morphology and syntax of Kalaḅarị I will discuss here are those that have direct relevance to tone. A full account of morphosyntactic phenomena in Kalaḅarị is given in Jenewari (1977). My analysis of the syntax of Kalaḅarị will be presented within the proposals of the Government and Binding framework (henceforth GB), Haegeman (1997) and references cited there, and Radford (1997), adopting as far as possible the non-controversial aspects of the theory. The following paragraph summarizes the basic assumptions of the theory.

GB provides a modular approach to the syntactic organization of linguistic elements in languages. The modules include X-bar theory, Case theory, Binding, Bounding, and Theta theories. I adopt X-bar theory for providing basic descriptions of the relevant syntactic structures of Kalaḅarị. The basic assumption of X-bar theory is that the kinds of relationships within constituent constructions are defined by universal principles. In X-bar theory, the heads of syntactic constituents may belong to a lexical category (Noun, Verb, Adjective, etc.) or a functional category (INFL, DET, etc.). Syntactic structures such as phrases, clauses, etc. are seen as projections of the head. By implication, a noun phrase is headed by a noun, a verb phrase by a verb, etc.[9]

1.6.1 Classification of Kalaḅarị Morphemes

Kalaḅarị is largely an isolating language.[10] Nearly all morphemes are free, but there is a small class of bound morphemes. It is against this background that we will distinguish the morphemes into two categories, lexical and grammatical morphemes.

[9] Readers are referred to Haegeman (1997) and Radford (1997) for details of these and other notions in GB.

[10] The use of this term implies that words in Kalaḅarị are mostly monomorphemic. There is little morphology in Kalaḅarị, other than some tonal phenomena, e.g. the HL suffixal tones of the imperative, gerund HL, etc.

1.6.1.1 Lexical Morphemes

Lexical morphemes include nouns, verbs and adjectives. These items have both tonal and segmental specifications, as illustrated in (19). To the best of my knowledge, there are two adjectives in Kalaḅarị.

(19) a.	námá	noun (N)	'meat/animal'
b.	sìrá	verb (V)	'spray'
c.	kálá	adjective (A)	'small'
d.	ɔ́pú	adjective (A)	'big'

1.6.1.2 Grammatical Morphemes

Grammatical morphemes include pronouns, demonstratives, determiners and Tense/Aspect/Negation markers. Some of these morphemes too have both tonal and segmental specifications. The data in (20) illustrate.

(20) a.	ìnà	pronoun (Pro)	'their(s)'
b.	mí	demonstrative (Dem)	'this'
c.	mɛ́	determiner (Det)	'the'
d.	árì	Tense-Aspect (TAN)	'continuative'

Other grammatical morphemes have defective specification at either the segmental or tonal level. Toneless grammatical morphemes include the plural numeral modifier **-a** that also functions as plural marker, and genitive markers, **ɓa** 'daughter of' and **je** 'son of'. The toneless morphemes acquire surface tone by rightward tone spread from the syllable to the left, as illustrated in (21a). On the other hand, tonal grammatical morphemes include the H melody that marks gerund and the HL melody that marks causative and imperative. These morphemes never occur in initial position in the phrase. The examples in (21b) illustrate. In (21b), the only vowel is either doubled or tripled in order to receive the tonal morphemes on the surface (details of tone processes are given in Chapters 2 & 3).

(21) a. Toneless morphemes

-a as in íní + a	[íníá]	'four' pl. modifier
ɓa as in gógò + ɓa	[gógòɓà]	'daughter of Gogo'
ɓa as in kúrú + ɓa	[kúrúɓá]	'daughter of Kuru'
je as in kúrú + je	[kúrújé]	'son of Kuru'

b. Tonal morphemes

HL as in sɔ + H-Gerundive [sɔ̀ɔ́] 'cooking'
námá sɔ̀ɔ́ mɛ́ ìɓí꜌ḿ
meat cook-H Det good-completive 'the meat cooking is good'

HL as in sɔ + HL-causative [sɔ̀ɔ́ɔ̀] 'cause to cook'
námá s sɔ̀ɔ́ɔ̀ mɛ́ ìɓí꜌ḿ
meat cook-HL Det good-completive 'to cook meat is good'

HL as in sɔ + HL-Imperative [sɔ́ɔ̀] 'cook!'
ɓùrù sɔ́ɔ̀
yam cook-HL 'cook yam!'

1.6.2 Basic Word Order

The basic constituent order in a simple sentence is Subject-Object-Verb (SOV) in Kalaḅarị, as shown in (22) below. The illustrations in this section are marked to show the surface tone patterns of items in the constructions.

(22) Word order in Kalaḅarị
bòmá wá꜌rí múárì
Boma house go-ASP 'Boma is going home'

The heads of the syntactic structures in Kalaḅarị are items of the classes N (noun), V (verb), Det (determiner) and INFL (inflection). Heads, be they lexical or functional, are always phrase final. (23) below provides a list of the types of syntactic constructions in Kalaḅarị which will be considered in the following chapters.

(23) Syntactic types in Kalaḅarị
a. $[_{NP}$ SPEC N]
b. $[_{VP}$ NP V]
c. $[_{DP}$ NP Det]
d. $[_{IP}$VP INFL]

(23) shows that the head of the phrase in each case appears rightmost in its domain, preceded by its complement and other specifiers. Specifiers of N in (23a) include possessors, demonstratives and quantifiers, all of which precede the head N. In (23b), an NP complement precedes the verb. Similarly, in (23c,d) the determiner is preceded by the NP, tense/aspect (INFL) is preceded by the VP. Given that specifiers and complements precede the lexical or grammatical head, Kalaḅarị may be classified as a left-modifying or right-headed

language. In what follows, I will give the relevant X-bar features of Kalaḅarị syntactic structures listed in (23).

1.6.2.1 INFL (IP) Phrase

IP is the equivalent of the sentence (S) in the GB framework. The IP is a maximal projection of the head, I (inflection), which is a functional category. The I node provides the source for tense/aspect. The structure of IP given in (24) accounts for the sentence structure in (22) above.

(24) Structure of Kalaḅarị IP
$[_{IP}$ [SPEC] $[_{I'}$ [VP] I]]

IP immediately dominates the subject-NP in SPEC, while I', the intermediate or minimal projection of the head, immediately dominates VP. The VP is the complement of I. (25) lists the 'I' or tense/aspect markers that occur in Kalaḅarị.

(25) I- Markers in Kalaḅarị

árì	'continuative aspect'
tɛ́ꜜɛ́	'perfective aspect'
ḿ	'factative'
ɓà	'future'

The data in (26) illustrate the use of the markers listed in (25) within I'.

(26) Verb and I markers

$[_{I'}$ $[_{VP}$ ɓó] $_{I}$ árì]	'coming'
$[_{I'}$ $[_{VP}$ ɓó] $_{I}$ tɛ́ꜜɛ́]	'has come (perfective)'
$[_{I'}$ $[_{VP}$ ɓó] $_{I}$ ꜜḿ]	'came (past)'
$[_{I'}$ $[_{VP}$ ɓó] $_{I}$ ɓà]	'will come'

1.6.2.2 Verb Phrase (VP)

The VP is the maximal projection of the verb (V). A complement in the VP precedes V in Kalaḅarị as illustrated in (27).

(27) VP Structure in Kalaḅarị
$[_{VP}$ [SPEC] $[_{V'}$ [COMPLEMENT] V]]

In this study, we will restrict ourselves to cases where the complement of V is an Object-NP. The syntactic affinity between the NP in Complement position and the head is determined by V', the minimal projection. (28) gives examples of VP constructions with Object NP.

(28) a. [V' [NP námá] V pɛ́lɛ́]
meat cut 'cut meat'

b. [V' [NP gógò] V nàŋgá]
Gogo trample 'step on Gogo's (foot)'

c. [V' [NP ìndʒì] V pòló]
fish skin 'skin fish'

1.6.2.3 Determiner Phrase (DP)

In works such as that presented in Haegeman (1997: 21-22), the head properties of determiners are recognized. Determiners are therefore treated as functional heads of the determiner phrase (DP). The NP is thus seen as the complement of D. In Kalaḅarị, determiners occur following the NP, as seen in (23) above. I propose the DP structure in (29) to account for the syntactic relationship between the NP and postposed determiner in Kalaḅarị.

(29) Structure of Kalaḅarị DP
[DP [SPEC] [D' [NP] D]]

DP is the maximal projection, while D' is the minimal projection of the head, D. NP which is the complement of D is within the D' projection. The features of the head in (30a) mark agreement between NP and the postposed determiners. The nature of this agreement is shown in the behavior of determiners as demonstrated in (30b). Agreement involves gender distinctions in the singular but not in the plural. Details of the Kalaḅarị gender system can be found in Jenewari (1980:44-49).

(30) Features of DP

a. D'
|
D
AGR
+ Number
+ Gender

b. Postposed Determiners

mɛ́	'the'	(singular neuter)
má	'the'	(singular feminine)
ɓé	'the'	(singular masculine)
má	'the'	(plural)

The data in (31) below illustrate the use of postposed determiners in simple DPs.

(31) a. Singular

[$_{DP}$ [$_{D'}$ [$_{NP}$ wáꜜrɪ́] $_{D}$ mɛ́]]	'the house' (singular neuter)
[$_{DP}$ [$_{D'}$ [$_{NP}$ ɛ́rɛ́ɓɔ́] $_{D}$ má]]	'the woman' (singular fem.)
[$_{DP}$ [$_{D'}$ [$_{NP}$ òbȉrȉ] $_{D}$ ɓé]]	'the dog' (singular masc.)
[$_{DP}$ [$_{D'}$ [$_{NP}$ ójíɓɔ́] $_{D}$ ɓé]]	'the man' (singular masc.)

b. Plural

[$_{DP}$ [$_{D'}$ [$_{NP}$ wáꜜrɪ́] $_{D}$ má]]	'the houses'	(plural)
[$_{DP}$ [$_{D'}$ [$_{NP}$ érémè] $_{D}$ má]]	'the women'	(plural)
[$_{DP}$ [$_{D'}$ [$_{NP}$ òbȉrȉ] $_{D}$ má]]	'the dogs'	(plural)
[$_{DP}$ [$_{D'}$ [$_{NP}$ ójápʊ́] $_{D}$ má]]	'the men'	(plural)

According to my proposal, demonstratives, question-words (interrogatives) and possessive pronouns occur in SPEC of DP. The last two items, like the determiners, are marked for gender. The null symbol indicates an empty determiner heading the DP, as seen in (32).

(32) a. Possessive pronoun + Noun

[$_{DP}$ [$_{SPEC}$ ìnà] [$_{NP}$ [$_{N'}$ $_{N}$ɓúꜜrú]] Ø]	'their yam'
[$_{DP}$ [$_{SPEC}$ á] [$_{NP}$ [$_{N'}$ $_{N}$féꜜnɪ̂]] Ø]	'her bird'

b. Demonstrative + Noun

[$_{DP}$ [$_{SPEC}$ ɓɪ́] [$_{NP}$ [$_{N'}$ $_{N}$tʊ̀ɓɔ́]]Ø]	'this male-child'
[$_{DP}$ [$_{SPEC}$ má] [$_{NP}$ [$_{N'}$ $_{N}$tʊ̀ɓɔ́]]Ø]	'this female-child'

c. Question-words + Noun

[$_{DP}$ [$_{SPEC}$ tɔ̀] [$_{NP}$ [$_{N'}$ $_{N}$pȉrɪ̂]]Ø]	'which bush?'
[$_{DP}$ [$_{SPEC}$ tɔ̀] [$_{NP}$ [$_{N'}$ $_{N}$wàrɪ́]]Ø]	'which house?'

1.6.2.4 Noun Phrase (NP)

The Noun (N) heads the NP. As listed in (23), specifiers precede N. (33) below illustrates the structure of the NP in Kalaḅarị.

(33) NP Structure in Kalaḅarị
[$_{NP}$ [SPEC] [$_{N'}$ [Complement] N]]

The NP is the maximal projection of N, while N' is the minimal projection of the head. Modifying nouns and quantifiers occur in SPEC position of NP. The data in (34) illustrate simple NPs containing these types of specifiers.

(34) a. Noun + Noun

[$_{NP}$ [$_{SPEC}$ gógò] [$_{N'}$ $_{N}$wárɪ̀]]	'Gogo's house'
[$_{NP}$ [$_{SPEC}$ tɔ̃́jẽ́] [$_{N'}$ $_{N}$kánà]]	'Tonye's basket'

b. Numeral Quantifier + Noun

[$_{NP}$ [$_{SPEC}$ ínʲá] [$_{N'}$ $_{N}$wàrɪ̀]]	'four houses'
[$_{NP}$ [$_{SPEC}$ mà] [$_{N'}$ $_{N}$fènȉ]]	'two birds'

1.7 Summary

This chapter described aspects of the phonological, morphological and syntactic structures of Kalaḅarị relevant to this study. These descriptions will form the basis for the analysis of lexical and phrasal tones that follows.

2

Lexical Tonology

2.0 Introduction

This chapter is devoted to tonal specifications of morphemes in Kalaḅarị. About 1,393 monomorphemic items of 3,747 items were analyzed.[11] These items give a fair representation of all possible tone patterns in Kalaḅarị.

2.1 Kalaḅarị Tone System

Kalaḅarị employs a tone system with two basic tone levels. These tone levels are H(igh) and L(ow), (Jenewari 1977: 91, Williamson 1988: 253). In (35) below are examples of monosyllabic items with the two levels.

(35) a.	fí	H	'eat'
b.	fì	L	'death'

The two levels give rise to lexical contrast between items which otherwise have identical or similar segmental specifications. Lexical tone is realized on the surface when items occur in isolation, as in the monosyllabic pairs in (35) above and in bisyllabic pairs in (36)

[11] The data for the analysis are based on a corpus of data drawn from a manuscript of a dictionary of Kalaḅarị compiled by S. Owiye, a native speaker of Kalaḅarị, in conjunction with Kay Williamson and other members of the Rivers Readers Project at the Universities of Ibadan and Port Harcourt, respectively.

(36) a.	fìrí	L-H	'leak'	c.	ầjí	L-H	'break'
	fírí	H-H	'skin(v)'		ầjì	L-L	'egg'
b.	íkù	H-L	'cocoyam'	d.	ókù	H-L	'savings'
	íkú	H-H	'louse'		òpù	L-L	'big'

The contrast in lexical meaning in the word pairs in (36a) is signaled by the difference in tone levels in the first syllable of each of the two items. On the other hand, in (36b) the difference is found in the second syllable. The pairs in (36a) and (36b) constitute minimal pairs for purposes of determining contrastive tone levels in Kalaḅarị. We also see the lexical contrasts in (36c) and (36d). The pair in (36d) is a near-minimal pair. Here, there is a segmental difference in medial position which, however, cannot be the source of the tonal difference on the first syllable in that pair.

2.1.1 The Pitch Levels

Downdrift and downstep also occur in Kalaḅarị. In downdrift, the pitch level of alternating H-L tone sequences is progressively lowered. For example, two H tones in a sequence of H-L-H syllables are realized on different pitch levels; the second H tone is lower in pitch than the first H tone. In downdrift, the affecting L tone is present on the surface, as the data in (37) show.

(37) a.	ópùró	H-L-H	'shrimps'
b.	sùkúlù wárì	L-H-L-H-L	'school house'

In the forms in (37) the H tone following the initial H tone is phonetically on a different pitch level. The second H tone is lower in pitch than the first H tone. This pitch drop is due to the intervening L tone that lowers the following H tone by a process of assimilation.

In contrast to downdrift in (37), in downstep, words show a lowered H tone following another H tone. In the examples in (38) there is no surface L tone between the two H tones occurring in sequence.

(38) a.	káꜜrá	H-ꜜH	'complete'
b.	òɓùkúꜜló	L-L-H-ꜜH	'back'

A pitch drop occurs on the second H tone in (38), though a L-toned syllable does not occur separating the two H tones. The second H tone, the one that is downstepped in (38), is phonetically like the second H tone in the H-L-H sequence in (37). This suggests that H -ꜜH is really H-L-H with a floating L tone. It can be concluded therefore that there is a L tone following the first H tone, which does not surface but which affects the following H tone. I propose the same analysis for both downdrift and downstep in Kalaḅarị, namely that pitch lowering of a H tone is as a result of that H tone occurring as the second H tone in a H-L-H sequence.

The proposal made here for Kalaḅarị, that a floating L tone downsteps a following H tone if and only if a H tone precedes, is not true for all languages. For example, Bamileke-Dchang as described by Hyman (1985b), Pulleyblank (1986: 38), Clark (1992: 32), and Stewart (1992: 197) has both L-ꜜH and L-ꜜL. In Bamileke-Dchang, L-ꜜH and L-ꜜL contrast with L-H and L-L respectively.

This pattern of downstep is, however, unusual in the tone languages of the world. On the other hand, languages abound which share the phenomenon of downstepped H tone being produced by a floating L tone being wedged between two linked H tones, as is being hypothesized for Kalaḅarị. Such languages include Igbo, Tiv, Margi and Ga'anda (Goldsmith 1976: 56-70, Pulleyblank 1986: 33-37 and Kenstowicz 1994: 363).

2.1.2 Contour Tones

Phonetically rising and falling tones occur in Kalaḅarị. However, these only appear in items which have two contiguous syllables and in which the second syllable is V. The data in (39) illustrate.

(39) a. pùá LH 'split/divorce'
b. sóò HL 'go!'

(39a) can be interpreted as rising tone while (39b) is a falling tone. Every vowel constitutes a syllable nucleus and must bear a tone. The implication is that each vowel in a sequence constitutes a separate syllable. In Kalaḅarị, therefore, phonetically rising and falling tones have to be analyzed as sequences of level tones over two syllables.

2.1.3 Tone Bearing Unit in Kalaḅarị

As shown in (8) and repeated in (40) below, where a V is deleted in a VN sequence the N is reassigned to the nucleus, becoming syllabic in the process. This surface syllabic nasal takes on the tone left by the deleted V.

(40) îŋ͡mg͡bè ~ ŋ͡ḿg͡bè 'oyster'
H L H. L

Also, from (9), we know that an onsetless-V syllable is deleted phrase-internally with tone being reassigned in the process. Therefore, a simple and straightforward analysis can be given by the proposal that, in Kalaḅarị, tones are mapped to syllables,[12] which are the tone-bearing units (henceforth TBUs). An overview of what constitute TBUs in African languages is given in Odden (1995b: 448-452).

---

[12]The V slot or mora can also be argued for as possible TBUs, but this is beyond the scope of this study.

2.2 Surface Tone Patterns in Morphemes

Of the 1,393 items considered, twenty-seven surface tone patterns occur in monomorphemic items in Kalaḅarị. We will explore how these patterns are distributed in mono-, bi-, tri- and quadri- syllabic items. If one assumes an open choice of H tone or L tone on each syllable, the theoretically possible number of tone patterns without floating L tone would be 2^n, with n representing the number of syllables in an item.

2.2.1 Monosyllabic Items

Using the formula 2^n in which n = 1, there are theoretically two possible tone patterns on monosyllabic items. In fact, there are two attested surface tone patterns, namely, L and H. (41) shows examples of nouns and verbs with H and L tone patterns (see extended datasets M1 – M2 in Appendix).

(41) Surface Tone Patterns of Monosyllabic Nouns (N) and Verbs (V)

	Pattern	Item	Gloss
a.	L	sì	'bad' (V)
	L	sò	'sky/heaven' (N)
b.	H	sɔ́	'enter' (V)
	H	sɛ́	'(national) state' (N)

Functional items also occur with these patterns. (42) gives examples of pronouns (Pro) and determiners (Det).

(42) Surface Tone Patterns of Monosyllabic Functional Items

	Pattern	Item	Gloss
a.	L	ò	'he/his' (Pro)
	L	à	'I' (Pro)
b.	H	má	'the' (Det)
	H	ó	'your' (Pro)

2.2.2 Bisyllabic Items

Given that there are two tone levels, the expected number of patterns in bisyllabic lexical items, assuming H tone and L tone being able to occur on any of the two syllables, is four using the formula 2^n, where n = 2 syllables. In fact, there are five patterns. The additional pattern is H-ꜜH. The second H tone is downstepped as a result of an immediately preceding floating L tone, as in previous examples in (38). The five tone patterns are L-L, L-H, H-L, H-H and H-ꜜH, as illustrated in lexical items in (43) below. It should be noted that verbs are not attested with the HL pattern (see extended datasets B1 – B3 in Appendix).

(43) Surface Tone Patterns of Bisyllabic Lexical Items

	Pattern	Item	Gloss
a.	L-L	ìɓì	'good' (V)
		pìrì	'bush' (N)
b.	L-H	sìá	'split' (V)
		ìrí	'thread' (N)
c.	H-L	íkù	'cocoyam' (N)
d.	H-H	ɛ́rí	'see' (V)
		síɓí	'head' (N)
e.	H-ꜜH	déꜜkí	'carry' (V)
		ɓáꜜrá	'hand/arm' (N)

Functional items occur with three of these tone patterns as given in (44).

(44) Tone Patterns of Functional Bisyllabic Items

	Pattern	Item	Gloss
a.	L-L	ànì	'it/that'(Pro)
b.	H-H	tírá	'three' (Num)
c.	H-L	nínè	'eight' (Num)

2.2.3 Trisyllabic Items

The possible number of tone patterns for trisyllabic items using the formula 2^n (n = 3 syllables) will give eight tone patterns. The eight patterns, L-L-L, L-L-H, L-H-L, L-H-H, H-H-H, H-L-H, H-H-L and H-L-L, are attested in the database. However, three additional patterns occur, namely H-ꜜH-H, H-H-ꜜH and L-H-ꜜH, all involving downstep. Thus, the total number of tone patterns attested in trisyllabic items is eleven.

Two out of the eleven tone patterns, namely L-H-H and H-L-L, seem to be restricted. With two exceptions, they are found only in loan words. The total number of items with the L-H-H pattern is two, and they are of Igbo origin. Twenty items occur with the H-L-L pattern in the database. Of this number, twelve items are of Igbo origin and six items are of English origin.

The only attested trisyllabic functional items are the second and third person plural pronouns. It is these two which represent the only native items with the H-L-L pattern. Historically, however, these pronouns are complex, as proposed in Harry (1995: 158-159). For the purposes of this analysis, therefore, I will ignore them. The data in (45) will, as a result, only show attested surface tone patterns of trisyllabic native lexical items. The L-H-H and H-L-L patterns are, as a consequence, not represented in this list (see the extended datasets T1 – T5 in the Appendix).

(45) Surface Tone Patterns of Trisyllabic Lexical Items

	Pattern	Item	Gloss
a.	L-L-L	ɪ̀ŋgùmà	'throw'
		àkàmà	'bee'
b.	L-L-H	ɪ̀kpèpú	'padlock'
		bèkèlé	'insane'
c.	L-H-L	àkpálɪ̀	'mat'
		àgíɾɪ̀	'masquerade'
d.	H-H-H	ókúró	'shoes'
		fóróró	'empty'
e.	H-H-L	ɛ́wɛ́lɛ̀	'fish sp.'
		pílámà	'bitter-leaf'
f.	H-L-H	ópùró	'shrimps'
		pékèlé	'turn'
g.	H-H-ꜜH	ásáꜜná	'spray/sprinkle'
		ɓékéꜜké	'chin'
h.	H-ꜜH-H	íŋꜜgóló	'limpet'
		ɪ́ꜜrʊ́á	'sun'
i.	L-H-ꜜH	àdáꜜká	'rashes'
		sɪ̀káꜜká	'kapok'

2.2.4 Quadrisyllabic Items

Following the formula 2^4, sixteen theoretically possible tone patterns may be expected to occur in quadrisyllabic items. The sixteen possible tone patterns and the corresponding attested tone patterns in the database are listed in (46) below. The patterns in parenthesis are those associated with loan words.

(46) Surface tone Patterns of Quadrisyllabic lexical items

Theoretically Possible Patterns		Attested Patterns	
L-L-L-L	H-H-H-H	L-L-L-L	H-H-H-H
L-H-L-L	H-L-H-H	(L-H-L-L)	
L-H-H-L	H-L-L-H		
L-L-H-L	H-H-L-H	L-L-H-L	H-H-L-H
L-L-L-H	H-H-H-L	L-L-L-H	H-H-H-L
L-L-H-H	H-H-L-L		
L-H-L-H	H-L-H-L	L-H-L-H	H-L-H-L
L-H-H-H	H-L-L-L		(H-H-L-L)
8 + 8 = 16		5+ 5 = 10	

As seen from (46) above, only ten out of the sixteen possible surface tone patterns are attested. Of these ten tone patterns, two, L-H-L-L and H-H-L-L, are associated only with items of English origin and will, therefore, be excluded for purposes of this analysis. In addition, two surface tone patterns involving downstep occur, L-L-H-ꜜH and H-L-H-ꜜH, to give a total of ten tone patterns for native quadrisyllabic lexical items.

Lexical and functional items are listed in each pattern. However, there are no functional quadrisyllabic items. The data in (47) below provide examples of tone patterns in native quadrisyllabic lexical items (see extended datasets Q1-Q5 in Appendix).

(47) Surface Tone Patterns of Quadrisyllabic Lexical items

	Pattern	Item	Gloss
a.	L-L-L-L	àkòŋgòɓà	'firefly'
		ìgùrùbè	'locust'
b.	L-L-L-H	àgbàkùrú	'bucket'
		ìkèlèmá	'round'
c.	L-L-H-L	èdʒìmínà	'ram'
		ɪ̀gùáŋgɪ̀ (archaic)	'money'
d.	L-H-L-H	òlómìní	'lime'
		àkírìmá	'game of tops'
e.	H-H-H-H	ágɓágárá	'wood sp.'
		íkíríkó	'drum'
f.	H-H-H-L	íkúlélè	'iron'
g.	H-H-L-H	ófógòró	'empty'
h.	H-L-H-L	ɔ́kìríngà	'harmattan'
		élèlíà	'fish sp.'
i.	L-L-H-ꜜH	òɓùkúꜜló[13]	'back'
j.	H-L-HꜜH	óɓùlóŋꜜgó	'African darter'

2.2.5 Summary of Surface Tone Patterns

Attested tone patterns for items of up to four syllables in length are the focus of this analysis. This is because items of five or more syllables rarely occur. Such items found in the entire corpus accounted for only 0.86% of the database. Most of these are bimorphemic compounds, reduplications etc. and, as a consequence, are not of interest for the purposes of the current analysis.

Against this background, we may distinguish two main classes of tone patterns in Kalaḅarị. These are (i), patterns without floating L tone, and (ii), patterns with floating L tone. In the former, all tones surface on syllables, whereas in the latter, a L tone floats which induces downstep on a following H tone, if any, as earlier discussed in §2.1.1.

[13]The status of this item as a single underived lexical item is in doubt (see comment in (Q5) in Appendix).

The number of theoretically possible patterns generated by 2^n would be thirty, 2 + 4 + 8 + 16 = 30. Of this number, the total of the patterns without floating L tone actually attested is twenty, 2+4 + 6 + 8 = 20. There are, in addition, six patterns involving floating L tone, i.e. H$^{\downarrow}$H on bisyllabic items, HH$^{\downarrow}$H, H$^{\downarrow}$HH, LH$^{\downarrow}$H on trisyllabic items and HLH$^{\downarrow}$H, LLH$^{\downarrow}$H on quadrisyllabic items. There are, therefore, twenty-six attested surface tone patterns in native items, as shown in the table in (48) below.

(48) Summary of Attested Surface Tone Patterns

Mono	Bi	Tri	Quad	T/Pattern
L	L-L	L-L-L	L-L-L-L	4
-	L-H	L-L-H	L-L-L-H	3
-	-	L-H-L	L-L-H-L	2
H	H-H	H-H-H	H-H-H-H	4
-	H-L	H-H-L	H-H-H-L	3
-	-	H-L-H	H-H-L-H	2
-	-	-	H-L-H-L	1
-	-	-	L-H-L-H	1
	H-$^{\downarrow}$H		H-L-H-$^{\downarrow}$H	2
-	-	H-H-$^{\downarrow}$H H-$^{\downarrow}$H-H	-	2
-	-	L-H-$^{\downarrow}$H	L-L-H-$^{\downarrow}$H	2
2	5	9	10	26

There is a significant discrepancy between the number of possible tone patterns as generated by 2^n, thirty, and the number of actually occurring tone patterns without floating L tone, twenty. This suggests that we could not assume that in Kalaḅarị, there was freedom to mark each available syllable as bearing either H or L tone. The restricted number of actually attested patterns points to the possibility that they may be generated by a limited number of underlying tone melodies.

2.3 The Analysis of Kalaḅarị Tone

In this section we present the analysis of the underlying melodies and their corresponding surface distribution within aspects of three complementary approaches to phonology, namely, Lexical Phonology (LP), Autosegmental Phonology and CV Phonology.

2.3.1 Lexical Phonology

Lexical Phonology was first proposed by Kiparsky (1982, 1985). It was further developed by Mohanan (1982, 1986). LP was proposed to account for the dependencies that exist between phonological processes and morphological processes, on one hand, and the levels or strata of rule application in a language, on the other hand. Since Kiparsky and Mohanan, many other versions of LP have been proposed. Pulleyblank (1986) extended the theory to the study of tone. The general assumptions of LP in all of the versions in the literature are very similar. Rules may apply in two main components of the phonology, the lexical and the post-lexical. Lexical rules are restricted to word-formation processes in the lexicon, while post-lexical rules apply in syntactic processes and always follow all lexical rule applications.

2.3.2 Autosegmental Phonology

Pulleyblank's LP theory of tone, in addition to the above properties incorporates aspects of Autosegmental Phonology (AP) as presented in Goldsmith (1976, 1990), and by others. Pulleyblank incorporated the basic notion from AP that tonal features are semi-autonomous from segmental features and should be represented on a separate tonal tier or separate tonal tiers. A tone language, in addition to possessing other tiers, will have a tonal tier. A formal phonological representation of a tone language will therefore show a consistent account of how tone is linked to its bearers on a separate tier. In AP, linking is established by non-crossing association lines. Pulleyblank (1986: 11, 78) proposes some universal aspects of tone mapping, as in (49), and adopts the well-formedness condition proposed by Goldsmith (1976: 27), which I present in (50) below.

(49) Association Convention
Map a sequence of tones onto a sequence of tone-bearing units
a. from left-to-right
b. in a one-to-one relation

(50) Well-formedness Condition (WFC):
Association lines do not cross

WFC is universally accepted, however, (49) has been enriched by the proposal by Yip (1988: 551) that languages may choose from three options for associating elements on parallel tiers: (i) left-to-right, as given in Pulleyblank (1986: 79-80) for Tiv, (ii) right-to-left association, as given by Newman (1986) for Hausa, and (iii) edge-in association, as presented by Black (1995) for Kinande.

Further, Pulleyblank (1986: 80-83) proposes that tone spread is derived by a language-specific rule. This represents a crucial difference from earlier proposals by Goldsmith (1976: 50) and Clements and Ford (1979: 187) who proposed a universal spreading rule.

2.3.3 CV Phonology

Clements and Keyser (1983) propose the syllable theory known as CV phonology, which is an outcome of AP. The theory proposes the existence of three tiers in the representation of the syllable, (i) syllable tier (σ-tier), (ii) the CV-tier, consisting of elements of C and V, and (iii) and segmental tier which consists of phonetic features that characterize the C and V. A well-formed syllable will be that in which the three tiers are linked by non-crossing association lines. Pulleyblank (1986: 14) proposes that the CV-tier coordinates the tone tier and any other tier in a phonological representation. It thus serves as a skeletal tier consisting of slots that are linked to elements on other tiers.

Although most phonologists currently assume that each phonological feature, whether segmental or tonal, is represented on its own tier, I adopt a simpler representation in addressing Kalaḅarị phonology. First, for expository reasons, I adopt a CV-tier to represent the skeleton which will bear both segmental and tonal material. Second, I treat all segmental features as if they were all on a single segmental tier. Third, I likewise represent tonal features such as L and H, for 'low' and 'high', on the same tier. Thus, for Kalaḅarị words such as **dàmá** 'confront' and **bélè** 'light' I use the following representations.

```
(51) a  d a m a          b.  b e l e        Segmental tier
        | | | |              | | | |
        C V C V              C V C V        CV-tier
          |   |                |   |
          L   H                H   L        Tone tier
```

However, it is equally possible to adopt a moraic representation such as that employed in Hyman (1985) and Hayes (1989).

2.3.4 Options for Representing Underlying Tones

One of the questions which has occupied the minds of researchers in tonology is how to provide the simplest, the most economical and revealing formal account which captures a native speaker's intuition about the underlying representation of tone in a language. Two proposals on the underlying representation of tone have been given in the literature on autosegmental phonology. These proposals capture two different strategies supposedly adopted by speakers of tone languages.

In one strategy tones are underlyingly unlinked to TBUs. Surface tone mapping is determined by rules and conventions. In the second strategy, tones are underlyingly linked to TBUs with every TBU having lexically assigned tone. The former is proposed to be that which is used in Mende as demonstrated in Leben (1980) and in Igbo as shown in Goldsmith (1979). The latter is supposedly used in Yoruba, as suggested by Pulleyblank (1986).

The two strategies are by no means exclusive, as studies such as that of Pulleyblank (1986) on Yoruba have shown that languages can combine the two strategies. The application of these strategies depends on the language, or on the specific subpart of the language that motivates linked versus unlinked tones. Formally, an association line is used to show the linked tone in an underlying representation. I illustrate the application of the two strategies in (52) below.

```
(52) a. V C VCV    b. VCVCV      c. VCVCV   d. VCVCV
                      |                |              |
         H            H                H              H
```

If we assume that Kalaḅarị tones are underlyingly unlinked, (52a) will be the structure of underlying representations in Kalaḅarị. Then rules and conventions would be introduced to map a tone to its bearer to account for the surface representation. On the other hand, where we assume linked underlying representations, we have to choose from the other representations in (52). If we assume (52b) (52c) and (52d) underlyingly linked tones for Kalaḅarị, the following lexical representations in (53)[14] are possible for the item **ókúró** 'shoe' in which all the TBUs have surface H tone.

```
(53) a.  o k u r o       b. o k u r o      c. o k u r o
         |                      |                    |
         H                      H                    H
```

In this account the representations show that H tone may be underlyingly linked to any of the TBUs in the item. The choice here depends largely on some other fact such as the direction of tone spread. (53a) will require rightward spread, (53b) bidirectional spread and (53c) leftward spread. However, the selection of the appropriate tone spread rule presupposes an initial tone association. This brings us back to the decision on the proper linking in (52).

As compared with proposals in (52b,c,d), (52a) which assume that underlying tones are unlinked, **ókúró** would have just one representation. This underlying lexical representation is given in (54).

```
(54)     okuro
          H
```

As we already know from §2.2.5, the total number of possible tone patterns generated by 2^n is thirty (30), but the number of actually occurring surface tone

[14]The forms in (53b) and (53c) seem to be as in Japanese (Zubizarreta 1982)

patterns excluding those with floating L tone is twenty (20). The closer the number of surface tone patterns is to the number that can be generated by the formula, 2^n, the greater the justification for a lexical association of H/L to each syllable. Given the restricted number of attested patterns without floating L tone in Kalaḅarị, the proposal that the melody is assigned to the whole item is worth exploring. This is the line of inquiry that will be pursued here.

I assume, for purposes of my analysis, that where identical tones occur on immediately adjacent syllables following the Obligatory Contour Principle (OCP) (Leben 1973, 1980; Goldsmith 1979, 1990; Pulleyblank 1986, Odden 1995), there is only one tone underlyingly which spreads via a tone spread rule to the neighboring syllables bearing identical surface tone. Against this background, we proceed to identify the tone mapping conventions that will generate the twenty-six surface tone patterns.

2.4 Tone Mapping in Kalaḅarị

Given that it is being proposed here that underlyingly tones are not linked to TBUs in Kalaḅarị, tonal rules and conventions will be needed to determine the mapping of tones in tone melodies to TBUs. Three options for mapping of tones are available for speakers of tone languages to choose from. These options are (i) left-to-right, L→R, (ii) right-to-left, R→L, and (iii) edge-in association, EI.

Tone assignment in some languages adopts (i), L→R association. For example, Mende (Leben 1980; Odden 1995b:446-447) is analyzed as adopting a L→R association. The same is proposed for Tiv (Pulleyblank 1986:68-71). In addition, in these languages, tone spread, when it occurs, is rightwards. A L→R association is implemented by the association conventions in (55) below.

(55) Association Convention (AC)
Map a sequence of tones onto a sequence of tone-bearing units,
a. from left-to-right
b. in a one-to-one relation
c. associate the last linked tone rightwards to a free tone-bearing unit after (b).
d. associate the last tone-bearing unit with a tone left after (b).

In the examples in (56) below, I demonstrate how tones in a two-tone melody would be assigned to TBUs in Kalaḅarị following a L6R association. The examples **énémè** 'oil palm' and **ìkèlèmá** 'round' illustrate this association. We will assume underlying HL and LH melodies, respectively, for these items, as proposed in §2.5.1 below.

(56) a. b.

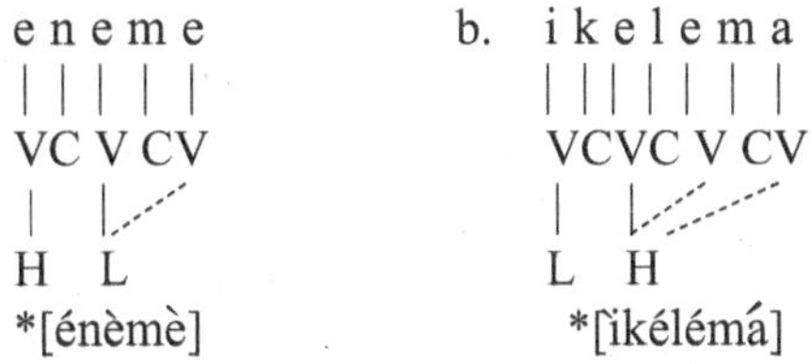

Seg-tier
CV-tier
AC + Spread
Output

Obviously, the forms in (56) show that a L→R association will predict ill-formed Kalaḅarị surface representations *HLL and *LHHH. L→R association convention is an option that cannot be adopted by Kalaḅarị. Kalaḅarị has LLH and HHL, but not *LHH and *HLL, and the analysis to be presented in this study accounts for this.

On the other hand, languages such as Hausa (Paul Newman 1986) adopt the second option, R→L association. In this case, tones are mapped from the right edge leftwards. In the event that an association runs out of free tones the last linked tone is associated to any TBU on the left not previously assigned a tone. In other words, tone spread is leftwards. I consider how this option will account for the Kalaḅarị examples in (57).

(57) a. b.

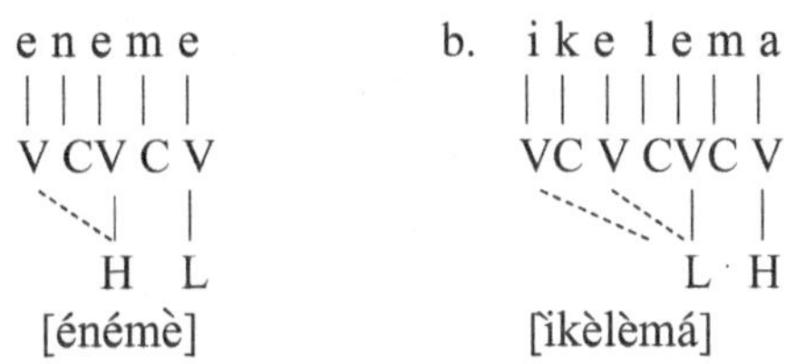

Seg- tier
CV-tier
R→L
Output

As seen from the forms in (57), the R→L association generates the acceptable outputs for Kalaḅarị. This suggests that speakers of Kalaḅarị may be using a R→L association convention in mapping tones to TBUs.

However, let us consider the last option, in which association is from the edges inwards, as presented in Yip (1988). According to this approach, the edge tones in a melody are associated with the edge TBUs, and the tones next to each edge to their corresponding TBUs.

When one runs out of tones any remaining TBU receives surface tone from the spread of the tone either leftward or rightward depending on the language. This is an option argued for in Bambara and Shona, as demonstrated in Kenstowicz (1994: 369-376) and references cited there. The Kalaḅarị examples given above are repeated in (58) below.

(58)

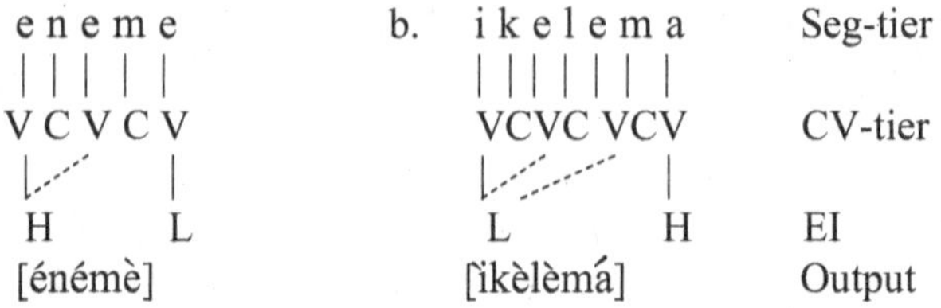

The forms in (58) show that association at the two edges plus rightward tone spread will predict acceptable representations of tone in Kalaḅarị. Thus, it appears that R→L and EI association with rightward spread are possible candidates for explaining surface tone association in Kalaḅarị. EI with leftward spread would produce an unacceptable pattern, *LHHH.

The data we examined above are the simple two-tone melodies, HL and LH. Consider further how R→L and EI associations would map tones in items with a sequence of three tones in the underlying melody. The illustrative data are **pékèlé** 'turn' and **èdʒìmínà** 'ram' for which I propose HLH and LHL melodies respectively. The derivations in (59) below show the results of R→L association plus leftward spread in (59b).

(59)

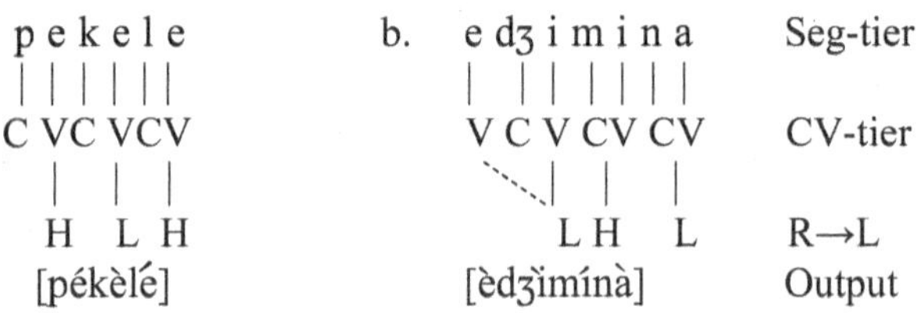

Now compare the derivations in (59) to those given in (60) below showing EI association.

(60)

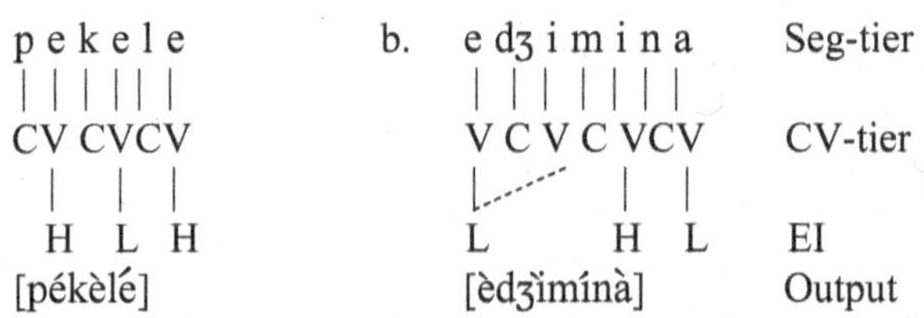

Note that in the application of EI, there is the option of assigning the H tone to the second syllable in the item. However, if H tone in (60b) is assigned to the second syllable it would then spread rightwards to the penultimate syllable, thereby generating an ill-formed representation, ***èdʒímínà.**

There are two language-specific parameters for EI association: (i) left-edge versus right-edge dominance and (ii), direction of spread, leftward or rightward spread. At the initial stage, the two edges are associated with the two edge tones. At the second stage of association, in a left-dominant EI association, a tone will be assigned to a syllable on the left, while in a right-dominant EI association, a tone is assigned to the syllable on the right. Tone spread is determined by (i).

For EI association to work in Kalaḅarị, a right-dominant version of EI association is the one that would have to be proposed. Therefore, to account for the correct output within this analysis, in (60b), at the second application of EI association, the H tone has been assigned to the penultimate syllable rather than the second syllable of the item, i.e. one has to apply a language-specific parameter in order for EI association to explain the Kalaḅarị data. However, no such similar language-specific parameter has to be invoked if one proposes R→L association for Kalaḅarị, as shown in (59b) above. The association of H tone follows from the general convention that in R→L association tones are mapped from the right. A R→L association, therefore, provides the simpler and more economical account of tone mapping in Kalaḅarị.

Goldsmith (1990:18) provides discussion of parametric settings across languages. In order to present a formal analysis of tone mapping in Kalaḅarị working with this Goldsmith model, I propose the following in (61) below. The numbers in braces indicate the lower and upper limits of associations between TBUs and tones and vice versa in Kalaḅarị.

(61) Kalaḅarị Tone Association

a. initial tone association occurs following a R→L mapping convention
b. one and only one TBU is associated per tone, TBU{1,1}
c. one and only one tone is associated per TBU, Tone{1,1}
d. when an association runs out of tones the last linked tone spreads to the remaining syllables to the left

Based on the proposals in (61), I will present rules and conventions in the following subsection which will provide an analysis of the relationship between the underlying tone melodies and their surface realizations in Kalaḅarị.

The facts of Kalaḅarị as presented above demand that we map tones to bearers on a parallel tier beginning from the right edge. (62) provides an initial tone association rule in Kalaḅarị. ']' indicates right-edge of the word.

(62) Initial Tone Association (ITA)
Map a tone to a right-edge TBU
...C_0 V]
  ⋮
  T

In addition, I propose that after the application of ITA (62), any remaining tone is associated in a one-to-one relation from right-to-left, following the R→L association convention in (63) below.

(63) Right-to-Left Association Convention (R→L association)
Map tones, /T_1T_2.../, in a melody, to TBUs as follows:
a. right-to-left
b. one-to-one relation

The R→L association proposed in (63) claims that mapping always starts at the right edge and reapplies when unassociated tones and TBUs still remain after ITA application. I will attempt in what follows to demonstrate how ITA interacting with R→L association applies to associate tones in underlying tone melodies to TBUs in Kalaḅarị.

As seen in the data given in §2.2, some of the tone patterns occur in items in which there are more TBUs than are tones. By my analysis, at the application of ITA, the right-edge tone will anchor to the right-edge TBU. Any additional TBUs receive remaining tones in a one-to-one relation following a R→L association convention. When unassociated TBUs remain after all tones are assigned, the last linked tone spreads to these units. The direction of tone spread is generally now considered to be language-specific (see §2.3.2). The rule in (64) below provides a language-specific tone spread rule in Kalaḅarị. This rule accounts for surface identical tones in a lexical tone pattern in Kalaḅarị.

(64) Tone-Spread (TS)
Spread a linked tone to a free TBU to its left.
V C_0 V]
 ⋱ |
   T

TS is an iterative rule which spreads a linked tone leftwards whenever an untoned TBU still remains after R→L association has completed its process of association. TS applies in order to satisfy a set of well-formedness conditions which scans the phonological representations after R→L association. The set of well-formedness conditions I propose for Kalaḅarị are given in (65).

(65) Well-formedness Conditions (WFC)

a. All TBUs are associated with a tone.

b. No TBU may be associated with more than one tone.

The WFC (65a,b) are conditions that are true for Kalaḅarị. What is also implied but not stated is the universal condition that association lines, i.e. the lines linking tone to TBU, do not cross. This is a well-established condition in AP and need not be repeated here (Goldsmith 1976: 27, 1990: 319). This last condition has the effect of ensuring that it is the leftmost tone in Kalaḅarị which is able to spread onto any remaining TBUs to the left. R→L and TS, triggered by the WFC (65), straightforwardly derive the surface tone patterns shown in the following subsections.

2.4.1 Tone Mapping in Patterns without Floating L tone

From (48), we observed that twenty-five surface tone patterns occur in Kalaḅarị. I repeat these patterns in (66) below.

(66) Surface Tone Patterns

Mono	Bi	Tri	Quad	T/ Pattern
L	L-L	L-L-L	L-L-L-L	4
-	L-H	L-L-H	L-L-L-H	3
-	-	L-H-L	L-L-H-L	2
H	H-H	H-H-H	H-H-H-H	4
	H-L	H-H-L	H-H-H-L	3
-	-	-	H-H-L-H	1
-	-	H-L-H	H-L-H-L	2
-	-	-	L-H-L-H	1
	H-ꜜH	H-H-ꜜH	H-L-H-ꜜH	3
-	-	H-ꜜH-H	-	1
-	-	L-H-ꜜH	L-L-H-ꜜH	2
2	5	9	10	26

Given that OCP, ITA and R→L association will account for the entire process of tone association in Kalaḅarị, I propose nine underlying tone melodies that account for the surface patterns seen in (66) above. These melodies are given in (67) below. The underlined 'L' indicates floating low tone.

(67) Underlying Tone Melodies (U-m)

Surface Pattern				U-m
Mono	Bi	Tri	Quad	
L	L-L	L-L-L	L-L-L-L	L
H	H-H	H-H-H	H-H-H-H	H
	H-L	H-H-L	H-H-H-L	HL
	L-H	L-L-H	L-L-L-H	LH
		L-H-L	L-L-H-L	LHL
	H-L̲-H	H-L̲-H		HLH
			H-L-H-L	HLHL
		L-H-L̲-H	L-H-L-H L-L-H-L̲-H	LHLH
			H-L-H-L̲-H	HLHLH

Eight tone melodies, L, LH, LHL, LHLH, H, HL, HLH and HLHL, generate patterns without a floating L tone if we assume R6L association. 84.48% of items in the corpus of data occur with surface tone patterns which can be straightforwardly derived from these melodies. (68) illustrates the distribution of surface tone patterns and the eight underlying melodies from which they are derived.

(68) Tone Melodies in Patterns without Floating L tone

Surface Pattern				U-m	Total%
Mono	Bi	Tri	Quad		D'base
L	L-L	L-L-L	L-L-L-L	L	30
H	H-H	H-H-H	H-H-H-H	H	29.09
	L-H	L-L-H	L-L-L-H	LH	15.41
	H-L	H-H-L	H-H-H-L	HL	5.8
		L-H-L	L-L-H-L	LHL	1.78
		H-L-H		HLH	0.9
			L-H-L-H	LHLH	0.5
			H-L-H-L	HLHL	1.0
2	4	6	7	8	84.48

Let us now look in detail at how specific melodies are mapped onto their TBUs in Kalaḅarị. We will first deal with single tone melodies, L and H. The illustrative data are **ɓèrì** 'ear', **ètèmì** 'tail' and **ìgùrùbè** 'locust' in (69), and **námá** 'animal/meat', **ókúró** 'shoe' and **íkíríkó** 'tom-tom' in (70). In the derivations in (69) and subsequently, UR represents underlying representation. In (69) are presented derivations representing items with an underlying L tone melody.

(69)

	a.	b.	c.	
	ɓeri	e t e m i	i g u rube	
	CVCV	VCVCV	VCVCVCV	
	L	L	L	UR
	ɓeri	e t e m i	i g u rube	
	CVCV	V C V CV	VCVCVCV	
	|	|	|	ITA
	L	L	L	
	ɓeri	e t e m i	i g u r u be	
	CVCV	V C V C V	V C V CVCV	
	⋱|	⋱⋱|	⋱⋱⋱|	TS
	L	L	L	
	[ɓèrì]	[ètèmì]	[ìgùrùbè]	

In (70) are items with underlying H tone melody.

(70)

	a.	b.	c.	
	nama	o k u r o	i k i r i k o	
	CVCV	VCV CV	VCVCVCV	
	H	H	H	UR
	nama	o k u r o	i k i r i k o	
	CVCV	V C V CV	VCV CV CV	
	|	|	|	ITA
	H	H	H	
	nama	o k u r o	i k i r i k o	
	CVCV	V C VCV	VCV CV CV	
	⋱|	⋱⋱|	⋱⋱⋱|	TS
	H	H	H	
	[námá]	[ókúró]	[íkíríkó]	

From the above, I propose that after the sole tone in a melody containing just one tone is assigned to the right-edge syllable by ITA, TS applies spreading that tone leftwards onto all the preceding syllables.

Now for melodies containing more than one tone, the derivations in (71), (72) and (73) below show the results of the application of ITA, R→L and TS in the following items with polytonic melodies: **nínè** 'eight' and **énémè** 'oil-palm', **bèkèlé** 'insanity', **àgbàkùrú** 'bucket', **àgírì** 'masquerade' and **èdʒìmínà** 'ram', respectively with HL, HL, LH, LH, LHL and LHL melodies.

```
(71) a.  n i n e              b.  e n e m e
         CVCV                     V CVCV
         HL                       HL                UR
         n i n e                  e n e m e
         CVCV                     V CVCV
            |                          |
          H L                        H   L          ITA
         n i n e                  e n e m e
         CV CV                    V CV  CV
          |  |                       |   |
          H  L                       H   L          R→L
                                  e n e m e
                                  V CV  CV
         N/A                       `..|   |
                                     H   L          TS

         [nínè]                   [énémè]           Output
```

In both (71a) and (71b), ITA applies to map the right-edge L tone. Then R→L association assigns the H tone to the next untoned syllable from the right. TS applies in (71b) to spread the H tone leftwards to give surface tonal realization to the remaining untoned syllable.

Consider now the derivation as it applies to LH melody in (72) below.

```
(72) a.  b e k e l e          b.  a gb a k u r u
         CVCVCV                   V C V CV CV
         LH                       LH                    UR
         b e k e l e              a gb a k u r u
         CVCVCV                   V  C V CV C V
               |                              |         ITA
           L   H                          L   H
         b e k e l e              a gb a k u r u
         CV  CVCV                 V C V CV CV
              |  |                         |   |        R→L
              L H                          L   H
         b e k e l e              a gb a k u r u
         C V CV CV                V  C  VC V CV
           `..|  |                 `.....`..|   |       TS
              L H                           L   H
         [bèkèlé]                 [àgbàkùrú]            Output
```

As in the derivations in (71) above, ITA and R→L assign the tones to syllables beginning from the right-edge. TS then spreads the last linked L tone leftwards onto the syllables to the left. This, therefore, accounts for the surface tone patterns in the derivations.

Let us now consider the derivation for LHL melody as it occurs in tri- and quadri-syllabic items.

```
(73) a. a g i r i          b. e dʒ i m in a
        VCVCV                 V C VCVCV
        LHL                       LHL              UR
        a g i r i              e dʒ i m in a
        VCVCV                 V  CVCVCV
            |                          |
         LH  L                  L  H     L         ITA
        a g i r i             e dʒ i m in a
        VCVCV                 V CV CVCV
        |  |  |                    |   |  |
        L  H  L                    L   H  L        R→L
                              e dʒ i m in a
        N/A                   V C VCVCV
                                ` ` ` ┘   |  |
                                   L   H  L        TS
        [àgírì]               [èdʒìmínà]           Output
```

Tone association in the derivations above follows ITA and R→L association. The identical L tone on the first and second syllables can be accounted for by TS that spreads the L tone, the leftmost tone, leftwards to the first syllable.

In the next set of data, we will consider the derivations of the following melodies: HLH, HLHL and LHLH. All the items with these melodies show equal number of tones to TBUs on the surface and we, therefore, do not have to invoke TS for these items. The data given in the derivations in (74) are **ópùró** 'shrimps', **ópùrópò** 'pig' and **òsíkìrí** 'sugar'.

(74)	a.	b.	c.	
	opuro	opuropo	osikiri	
	VCVCV	VCVCVCV	VCVCVCV	
	HLH	HLHL	LHLH	UR
	opuro	opuropo	osikiri	
	VCVCV	VCVCVCV	VCVCVCV	
	|	|	|	
	H L H	H L H L	L H L H	ITA
	opuro	opuropo	osikiri	
	VCVCV	VCVCVCV	VCVCVCV	
	| | |	| | | |	| | | |	
	H L H	H L H L	L H L H	R→L
	[ópùró]	[ópùrópò]	[òsíkìrí]	Output

In this set of cases, ITA associates the rightmost tone to the rightmost syllable. R→L association then assigns the preceding tones to syllables in a one-to-one relation from right-to-left.

2.4.2 Tone Mapping in Patterns with Floating L Tone

Five of the nine tone melodies, HL, HLH, LHL, LHLH and HLHLH, generate items with a floating L tone. These patterns account for 14.73% of items in the corpus of data. This percentage is quite significant. Generally, in patterns with floating L tone, the downstepped H tone induced by the floating L tone appears on the final syllable. However, there exists an exception in a subset of trisyllabic items, where downstep appears on the penultimate syllable rather than the final syllable.[15]

2.4.2.1 Patterns with Floating L Tone before Final Syllable

In the first set of cases the floating L tone does not occur as the final tone in the melody, and, as a consequence, induces downstep in the following H tone. I begin with derivations of items with HLH melody in which downstep occurs on the final syllable. The illustrative data are **fúꜜrá** 'be pregnant' and **ɓékéꜜké** 'chin'.

[15]Only a few trisyllabic nouns (three) were attested in the database with this exceptional pattern. Further, it is found in trisyllabic verbs which are transitive counterparts of some intransitive verbs with LH pattern (Jenewari 1980:25). The behavior of this pattern in the verbs suggests a complex derivational history which is beyond the scope of this study. The analysis given here is tentative. However, it will become part of further research on Kalaḅarị tone, as more data become available.

(75)

	a.	b.	
	f u r a CVCV HL H	ɓ e k ek e C VCVCV HL H	UR
	f u ur a CVVCV | H L H	ɓe k e ek e CVCVVCV | H LH	ITA
	f u ur a CVVCV | | | H L H	ɓ e k e ek e C VCVVCV | | | H L H	R→L
	N/A	ɓ e k e ek e CVCVVCV \\\| | | H L H	TS
	f u r a CVCV | | HLH	ɓe k e ke CVCV CV \\\| | HL H	V-deletion
	[fúꜜrá]	[ɓékéꜜké]	Output

The L tone associated with the deleted V floats, producing surface downstep in the final syllable. Consider now the derivations of LHꜜH pattern. This is derived from LHLH melody. The examples used are **ɔ̀ɓɔ́ꜜkɔ́** 'fowl' and **òɓùkúꜜló** 'back'.

```
(76) a. ɔ ɓ ɔ ɔ k ɔ          b. o ɓ u k u u lo
        VCVV C V                V CV CV VCV
        LHLH                    LHLH               UR
        ɔ ɓ ɔ ɔ k ɔ             o ɓ u k u ul o
        V CVVCV                 V C VCVVCV
              |                          |
         L H L  H                  L   H LH        ITA
        ɔ ɓ ɔ ɔ k ɔ             o ɓ u k u ul o
        V C VVCV                V C V CVVCV
        |    | |  |                |    | |   |
        L    HL  H                 L   H L  H      R→L
                                o ɓ u k u ulo
                                V C V CV VCV
        N/A                      ⋱|   |  |  |
                                L   H  L  H  TS

        ɔ ɓ ɔ ɔ k ɔ             o ɓ u k u l o
        V C V  CV               V C V C VCV
        |     |   |              ⋱|    |  |
        L    H L H                 L   HLH         V-Deletion
        [ɔ̀ɓɔ́ꜜkɔ́]                  [òɓùkúꜜló]         Output
```

Consider further the case of one item with HLHꜜH pattern derived from the HLHLH melody in (77) below.

```
(77)    o ɓ u l o oŋg o
        V CVCV VCV
        HLHLH                UR
        o ɓu lo oŋg o
        V CVCVVCV
                   |
        H   L  HL   H        ITA
        o ɓ u lo oŋg o
        V C VCVVCV
        |    |   | |   |
        H    L  H L H        R→L
        o ɓ u l o ŋg o
        V  CV CVC V
        |    |    |    |
        H   L    H L H       V-Deletion
        [óɓùlóŋꜜgó]          Output
```

Given the derivations above, we can see that ITA and R→L associate the underlying HLH, LHLH and HLHLH tones in a one-to-one relation moving from the right-edge. Then TS applies spreading the leftmost linked tone to the syllable on the left in (75b) and (76b). Finally, the penultimate V is deleted according to (7a), causing the L tone to float. The output shows a downstepped H tone on the final syllable, an effect from the floating L tone which precedes. Therefore, assuming a V-syllable that is deleted on the surface by the vowel deletion rule, we can straightforwardly derive those patterns which show downstep on the final syllable.

The proposal that these items do have underlying V-V sequence seems arbitrary, but there is at least a case in the language that appears to support this position. For example, some native speakers pronounce the word **òkóòkó** 'parrot' as **òkóꜜkó**. In this case, the deletion of the second V in the V-V sequence and the floating L tone bring about downstepping of the following H tone. Although, this evidence is not sufficient, it is necessary as a piece of evidence for the V-V analysis.

2.4.2.2 Patterns with Floating L Tone before Penultimate Syllable

As noted above, some surface trisyllabic items with HLH melody exhibit further exceptional behavior. In this class of items the penultimate syllable rather than the final syllable shows downstep. Given our analysis that all items with floating L tone have an extra underlying V syllable, these items would be underlyingly quadrisyllabic.

We know that ITA assigns the rightmost tone to the rightmost syllable. This explains downstep on the final syllables in the examples considered above. In the cases with downstep on the penultimate syllable, it seems that ITA assigns H tone to the penultimate syllable. The implication is that ITA ignores the final syllable in these items.

This phenomenon occurs in other languages. Pulleyblank (1986: 198-203) has shown that such a syllable at the periphery of a domain may be extratonal, i.e. it is not available for tone association until later in the derivation, because it is lexically marked [+extratonal]. He found this to occur in Margi. Following Pulleyblank, I propose extratonality, besides vowel deletion, to account for items with downstep on the penultimate syllable in the word.

Consider the derivations for **ɪ́ꜜrʊ́á** 'sun' and **íŋꜜgóló** 'limpet' in (78) below. I assume that the final syllable is extratonal, thus the rightmost H tone, skips it at the application of ITA.

```
(78) a. ɪ ɪr ʊ a             b. i iŋg o l o
        VVC V<V>                VVC V <CV>
        HL H                    HL H            UR
        ɪɪr ʊ a                 i iŋg ol o
        VVC V<V>                VVCV<CV>
              |                      |
        HL    H                 H  LH           ITA
        ɪɪr ʊ a                 i iŋg ol o
        VVCV<V>                 VV V<CV>
        | |   |                 | | |
        H L  H                  H L H           R→L
        ɪ r ʊ a                 i ŋg olo
        VCVV                    VCVCV
        |   |/                  |   |/
        HLH                     HL H            V-Deletion

        [íꜜrʊ́á]                 [íŋꜜgóló]       Output
```

ITA and R→L association apply, linking the tones from right to left, ignoring the final extratonal syllable. The final syllable is unavailable because it is marked extratonal [+ex]. H tone spreads rightwards to the final syllable when it becomes visible later in the derivation. Therefore, both extratonality and vowel deletion have to be invoked to account for downstep on a penultimate syllable, whereas vowel deletion without extratonality accounts for downstep on a final syllable in (78). Both manifestations of downstep derive from an underlying HLH melody. The syllabic constraint invokes a phonological rule involving vowel deletion which is already known to be part of the grammar of Kalaḅarị. Downstep is therefore due purely to surface phonological adjustment at the syllable structure level.[16]

---

[16]Williamson (1988) proposes an alternative analysis of these downstep patterns. According to Williamson (1988: 270), downstep H tone may be accounted for by assuming that certain L tones between two H tones float (L_0), i.e. they do not associate with a syllable on the surface, because it is lexically marked as [+float]. Therefore, only the H tones are assigned following R→L association. Implicit in Williamson's analysis is an assumption that there are two types of L tones, a L tone which does not float, as generated in the correct representations, **pékèlé** and **òsíkìrí**, and a L tone which has a lexical marking [+ float], generating forms in (77) and (78). Obviously [+float] could not account for the contrast between trisyllabic items with penultimate downstep in (78) and trisyllabic items with final downstep in (79b). In addition, the [+float] L tone would have to be marked as floating immediately prior to the penultimate syllable as in **síꜜkírí** and to the final syllable as in **ɓékéꜜké**. I argue that the [+float] proposal is more complicated than the syllabic constraint analysis.

2.5 Analysis of Tonal Patterns Exclusive to Loanwords

We noted in §2.2.5 that of the thirty theoretically possible tone patterns without floating L tone, eleven do not occur with native items. Such patterns include L-H-H, H-L-L, L-H-H-H, L-H-H-L, L-L-H-H, L-H-L-L, H-H-L-L, H-L-L-L, H-L-L-H and H-L-H-H. These represent non-accidental gaps, i.e. they do not occur because they cannot be generated by the R→L association which is part of Kalaḅarị phonology.

Three of the prohibited patterns appear in loans. The three patterns are H-L-L, H-H-L-L, L-H-L-L. From the database we observe that English loans with the three patterns are larger in number than Portuguese or Igbo loans. English loans have a total of thirty-seven items, Igbo has twenty-one, while Portuguese has six.[17] My focus in the following analysis is therefore on English loans with the three patterns, H-L-L, H-H-L-L and L-H-L-L. The following data in (79) show examples of these tone patterns among loans from English.

(79) a. H-L-L
gáɗɪnì 'garden'

b. H-H-L-L
báíbʊ̀lʊ̀ 'bible'

c. L-H-L-L
bɪ̀láŋgɪ̀ɗɪ̀ 'silky cloth'

In (79), all the loans involve vowel insertion in Kalaḅarị when compared to the English original. A vowel is inserted to produce CV syllables as follows: (i) if a syllable in the English original ends in a consonant (CV-C), (ii) if the English original has a cluster of consonants (CV-CC, CCV-C etc.), except where such consonant cluster begins with a nasal (NC). The result of epenthesis is open syllables and no onset cluster.

Given the data above, it appears that Kalaḅarị interprets stressed syllables of English items as H-toned and unstressed syllables as L-toned. Notice that in the examples in (79), the unstressed vowels in the cognates and the added vowels always surface with a L tone. Here, it appears that we can account for multiple L tones via a low tone spreading rule.[18] My proposal is that some English loans words that have syllabic specifications violating Kalaḅarị phonology are re-

[17] I present partial lists of non-native items in 2.L1 and 2.L2 in the Appendix.

[18] On the other hand, there are cases where L-spreading will not work. For example, in **sùkúlù** 'school' the vowel, [u], is inserted to break up the onset CC-cluster, and again after the coda-C, since Kalaḅarị disallows closed syllables. Thus, it appears that an L tone is assigned by default, in this case. Therefore, a default L tone insertion rule will be required to explain the presence of the L tone in such items.

paired at the surface level through the insertion of a vowel which receives a L tone via spreading.

My analysis is as follows. Given the fact that most Kalaḅarị speakers also speak Nigerian Pidgin English[19] (NPE) (Jones 1963: 19), the English loans do not have their epenthetic vowels underlyingly, i.e. the items are underlyingly /gáɗɪ̀n/, /blángɪ̀d/ and /báíbʊ̀l/, the forms they would have in NPE. In addition, we will assume that primary stress in metropolitan varieties of English is here interpreted as H tone, while any following unstressed syllable is interpreted as bearing a L tone. This would produce a HL melody for these items. These tones are then assigned to syllables following regular R→L association in Kalaḅarị.

It is after this that the items are submitted to the phonology of Kalaḅarị which requires that a vowel be inserted to create a CV-syllable where necessary. The inserted vowel receives a L tone via spreading. To account for this, I propose a L tone spreading rule in (80) below.

(80) L Spread (L-S)

V C V

|.......

L

In (81) below, I give derivations of **gáɗɪ̀nɪ̀** 'garden', **blángɪ̀ɗɪ** 'cloth resembling blanket' and **báíbʊ̀lʊ̀** 'bible' following this proposal.

[19]The term Nigerian Pidgin English (NPE) as used here is equivalent to Jones (1963:19) use of the term 'trade English'.

```
(81) a. gadın          b. baıbul        c. blangıd
        CVCVC             CVVCVC           CCVNCVC
        HL                HL                 HL        UR
        gadın             baıbul           blangıd
        CVCVC             CVVCVC           CCVNCVC
           |                  |                  |
        H  L                H L            H     L     ITA
        gadın              baıbul          bılangıd
        CVCVC             CVVCVC           CVCVNCVC
         |  |                | |            | |    |
         H  L                H L            LH     L   RL
                           baıbul
                           CVVCVC              N/A
        N/A                 \| |
                             H L                       TS
        gadı nı            baıbu lu        bılangıdı
        CVCVCV            CV VCVCV          CVCVCVCV
         |  |                \| |            | | |
         H  L                H L             L H L     VI
        gadı nı            baıbu lu        bılangıdı
        CVCV CV            CVVCVCV         CVCVCV CV
         |  |/               \| |/           | | |/
         H  L                H L             L H L     L-S
        [gádìnì]          [báíbùlù]        [bláŋgìdì]  Out.
```

A proposal like this would not require any alteration to the R→L and associated tone rules already proposed for native words in Kalaḅarị. It would be consistent with the analysis that in Kalaḅarị apparent deviant surface tone patterns in items are a product of the effect of syllabification processes. However, the analysis given here is inconclusive. The issue of loan word tonology is intriguing and equally complex in the language. Further study is need in that area.

2.6 Summary

The analysis of tone in the lexicon of Kalaḅarị yields the following findings. First, the surface tone patterns found with native Kalaḅarị items are derived from nine underlying tone melodies which are combinations of the basic tone levels, L and H. Second, these melodies are characterized by tones which are not associated with syllables in the underlying representations of items. Third, in Kalaḅarị, the surface tone patterns are derived from their underlying melodies via R→L association and a leftward tone spread rule, when required.

Of the nine melodies, four melodies, HL HLH, LHLH and HLHLH, show items in which an L tone floats, as a result of vowel deletion in obedience to a syllabic constraint. In all these melodies consisting of more than two tones, the floating L tone induces downstepped H tone on the final syllable. In addition, we observe a restricted class of items with HLH in which downstepped H tone occurs on the penultimate syllable. This is accounted for by positing lexically assigned extratonality of the final syllable operating in addition to vowel deletion.

3

Phrasal Tonology

3.0 Introduction

What are the tonal processes that take place when words already bearing their lexical specification for tone are combined in phrasal contexts in Kalaḅarị? It is this that is now the focus of our attention in this Chapter.

3.1 Tone Reduction

In an earlier account, Jenewari (1977: 95-96) proposed that ạn item occurring in non-initial position in a phrase undergoes a tonal change in Kalaḅarị. A more recent study by Williamson (1988: 254) makes a rather more general claim for Ịjọ, stating that the '... pitch pattern of a group is chiefly determined by the class of the initial morpheme ...'

The group, according to Williamson (1988: 255), is a prosodic structure in which all but the first word in the phrase are in a weak position. She proposes that an item in a weak position undergoes a tonal change. The illustration in (82) below shows the relationship of items within the group.

(82) Structure of the Group (Williamson 1988: 255)

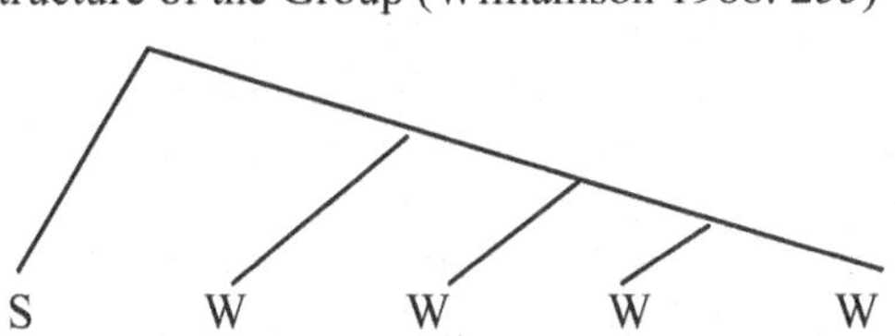

S = Strong
W = weak

Given the prosodic structure, 'strong . . . weak', in (82), the leftmost item, the tonal head (T-head) of the TG is **strong**, while any other item is in a **weak** position and thus loses its tones. In this, Williamson (1988:255) is most certainly correct. However, the question of whether the structure should be left-branching as she proposes or right-branching will be discussed in §3.5 below.

Williamson proposes a tone deletion process that ensures that an item in a non-initial or weak position becomes toneless. Second, she proposes that the deletion of the tone of the non-initial item triggers a number of tone rules which associate the tone of the leftmost item to following toneless syllables within the group, thereby accounting for tone changes in the group.

What is clear in both the proposals of Jenewari (1977: 95-96) and Williamson (1988: 255) is that non-initial items in a phrasal construction undergo some tonal change. In this chapter, I consider the tonal realizations that result from the deletion of non-initial tones within the group, as well as the nature of the group itself (continued in Chapter 4).

I propose, based on my own data and in keeping with Williamson (1988: 255) that in Kalaḅarị a lexically specified tone melody is deleted if the item with which it occurs occupies a non-initial position in the group. I present the Tone Deletion Rule (TD) in (83) below which effects this reduction in an item occurring in a non-initial position. After we have seen all the relevant data, a formal account of what constitutes a group will be provided in Chapter 4.

(83) Tone Deletion Rule (TD)

In a tone group, all items in a non-initial position delete their lexical tone.[20]

$[[W_1]\ [W_2]\ ...[W_N]]_{TG}$

```
 |    |      |
 T*   T*     T*
      ↓      ↓        W = Word
      Ø      Ø        T* = Any tone melody
```

It should be noted that there are two domains of tone assignment in Kalaḅarị, the lexical and the phrasal. The former must necessarily precede the latter. The TD rule deletes tones previously assigned to those lexical entries occurring in non-initial position in the phrase. The rule requires that tones be assigned to items in the lexicon before items are combined into phrases.

The structure created by TD triggers a rightward tone spread rule that spreads the lexically assigned tone melody of the initial item to following toneless syllables within the phrase. It was shown in Chapter 2 that at the lexical level, tone assignment was R→L and tone spread was leftwards. However, at the phrasal level the undeleted lexical tone melody is on the leftmost item and tone spread is rightwards, L→R. I propose a RTS tone spread rule in (84) below to account for tone spreading at the phrasal level.

[20]This pattern is similar to that found in Shanghai Chinese (Selkirk and Chen 1990).

(84) Rightward Tone Spread (RTS)
Spread a linked tone to a free TBU to its right within the TG.
V C_0 V]$_{TG}$
T

Let us now consider the application of TD in the example given in (85) below.

(85) a. a + ji ŋgi — 'her mother'
H L — Lexical Tone Assignment

a jiŋgi
H — TD

a jiŋgi
H — Tone spread

[á jíŋgî] — Output

It is clear that tones on the syllables of the non-initial item are reduced. The structure produced by TD triggers tone spread, spreading the H tone of the initial item rightwards onto the following syllables in the TG via RTS. Thus the pitch pattern of the TG, as seen above, is determined entirely by the tone of the first item.

However, there are many cases in which the lexical tone of the first item cannot alone explain the tone pattern of the TG. The examples in (86) below show that the lexically assigned tone melody of the initial item by itself cannot account for the surface patterns of the phrase.

(86)[21]a. be be + pi ri → [bébé pírì] 'whole bush'
H L → H L

b. tɔ + p ir i → [tɔ̀ pìrí] 'which bush?'
L L → L H

c. ɓuru + pir i → [ɓùrù pírì] 'yam's bush'
L L → L HL

d. ɪna + kʊkalɪ → [ɪ̀nà kʊ̀káꜝ ɪ́ɪ]²² 'their fish sp.'
L H LH → L HLH

In contrast to what seems to happen in the example in (85), in (86), there are respectively, L, H, HL and HLH melodies which appear on either the final syllable or the last two syllables of the non-initial item in the TG and which cannot be derived solely by spreading the lexical tone of the initial item. It seems, therefore, that the tone of the initial item is not always the only factor determining the surface tonal shape of the TG in Kalaḅarị.

Against this background, it is clear that in Kalaḅarị, surface tone patterns of TGs appear to be determined by either the lexical tone melody, henceforth TM_1, of the initial item only, or the TM_1 along with one of four tone melodies which are independent of the lexical tone melody. These tone melodies are L, H, HL, and HLH. The possible combinations are listed in (87).

(87) Surface Tone Patterns in TG
a. TP determined by TM_1
b. TP determined by TM_1 + L
c. TP determined by TM_1 + H
d. TP determined by TM_1 + HL
e. TP determined by TM1 + HLH

3.2 Tone Phrase Formation

As discussed earlier in §1.6.2, in Kalaḅarị, a syntactic phrase head occupies the rightmost position in the phrase. Syntactic modifiers thus precede the syntactic head. However, according to (82), prosodic headedness is to the left. Thus, assuming some correspondence between the TG and the syntactic phrases, a

---

[21] It appears that, like in lexical association, a right-to-left association can apply here to derive phrasal tones, as well. However, as we can see in (86d) and in other cases in the following sections of this chapter a right-to-left association will predict ill-formed representations in the phrasal tonology.

[22] An alternative acceptable pronunciation of (86d) will be [ɪ̀nà kʊ́kàɪ́ɪ]. In this case, L-spread is blocked allowing the L of the HLH melody to surface on the penult. This is a further piece of evidence supporting the proposal that HꜝH pattern derives from HLH melody in Kalaḅarị.

syntactic head in a TG formation in Kalaḅarị would tend to lose its lexical tone melody, since it would tend to occur to the right of its modifier in the TG.

While no identity exists in headship between TGs and syntactic phrases, the domain within which tonal headship operates nevertheless seems bounded by a syntactic head. Syntactic headedness defines the prosodic domain even though the syntactic head is not the strong member within that domain. Thus, a TG[23] is a prosodic structure bounded by a T-head on the left and a syntactic head on the right. In the following, we will see which syntactic heads are capable of defining such prosodic domains.

3.3 Effects of Morphological Class on Tone Phrases

In §3.2 above, I proposed that TD is a phrase level rule whose function is to delete the lexically assigned tone melody of items occurring in a non-initial position in the TP. In addition, I proposed that in some instances, additional tone melodies occur in TPs. These tone melodies are independent of the lexical tone melody of the initial item in the TP. In (88) I state the set of characteristics associated with a TP.

(88) Characteristics of a Tone Phrase

a. the leftmost item is the tonological head of the phrase, as it retains its lexical tone melody.

b. any other item within the TP following the leftmost item has its lexical tone melody deleted, by TD

c. some phrase types have a tone melody (L, H, HL or HLH).

Given (88a-b), it means that whenever an item retains its lexical tones it belongs to a separate TP from the item(s) which precede it. For instance, in the examples in (89) where serial verbs (V + V) are contrasted with a pronoun plus noun (Pro + N) sequence, we clearly see the effect of tone change on the latter, but not on the former.

(89) a. ɗȍsȉ + kóró → [ɗȍsȉ] [kóró] 'jump down'
V-V |/ |/ |/ |/ lit: jump get down
L H L H

b. á + j̏ìŋ gȉ → [á jíŋgí] 'her mother'
P+N | |/ |.../...
H L H

In the example in (89a), the lexically assigned tone melody of the second item is maintained, whereas in (89b) the tone is reduced, allowing the H tone from the first item to spread rightwards onto the following syllables of the second item. According to (88a-b) the first and the second items in (89a) belong to two separate TPs, whereas in (89b) the items belong to the same TP. In the following, we will consider the different types of two-word sequences in which tonal changes occur.

23 I will be using the equivalent term 'tone phrase (TP)' in this study.

3.3.1 Tone Phrases Determined by TM_1 Only

There is only one type of construction that falls into this class, namely, that of intimate possession, where the possessor is a pronoun. All pronouns behave in the TP the same, so it will suffice to illustrate with one H-toned and one L-toned possessive pronoun. Let us consider a set of NP constructions in which a H-toned possessive pronoun is followed by the intimate kinship nouns, **tà**, 'wife', **ɗì** 'husband', **ɗà** 'father' and **ǰìŋgì** 'mother', with lexically assigned L tone melody in (90).

(90) TP Determined by TM_1

	UR	TD	TS	Gloss
a.	í tà H L	í ta H	í tá H H	'your wife'
b.	á ɗì H L	á di H	á ɗí H H	'her husband'
c.	í ɗà H L	í ɗa H	í ɗá H H	'your father'
d.	á ǰìŋgì H L	á jiŋgi H	á jíŋgí H H H	'her mother'

The data above suggest an analysis involving deletion of lexical tone of the second item via TD (83) and the tone of the first item spreading rightwards via RTS (84) to the following word.

Consider further the examples in (91) in which the same kinship nouns, **tà** 'wife', **ɗì** 'husband', **ɗà** 'father' and **ǰìŋgì** 'mother', follow a L-toned possessive pronoun.

(91) TP Determined by TM_1

	UR	TD	TS	Gloss
a.	ɔ̀ tà L L	ɔ̀ ta L	ɔ̀ tà L L	'his wife'
b.	ì ɗì L L	ì di L	ì ɗì L L	'my husband'
c.	ɔ̀ ɗà L L	ɔ̀ ɗa L	ɔ̀ ɗà L L	'his father'
d.	ì ǰìŋgì L L	ì jiŋgi L	ì ǰìŋgì L L L	'my mother'

Crucially, the two sets of examples, (90) and (91), show that the tone on the second item must be identical to the tone of the first item in the surface representations of the phrases. TM_1 accounts entirely for the tone pattern in these cases.

The possessive pronoun plus intimate kinship noun construction given here is the only construction in which the surface tone pattern is entirely determined by TM_1. This construction differs in behavior from possessive pronoun plus non-intimate possessed nouns that we will consider in §3.3.3 below.

3.3.2 Tone Phrases with L Tone Melody

In Kalaḅarị, a L tone appears on the rightmost syllable of the second item in a two-item TP if the TP is made up of an NP in which the initial item is a quantifier. In this type of syntactic construction, the quantifier could be a non-numeral or numeral quantifier. We will discuss here only non-numeral quantifiers[24] (Quan). All non-numeral quantifiers followed by a noun generate the same surface tone patterns on the second item. A few examples will suffice to illustrate this. I begin in (92) with a H-toned quantifier followed by a noun.

(92) Quan + N Construction

	Quan + N	TD	TM_1 + L, RTS	Gloss
a.	bébé pȉrȉ H L	bébé piri H	bébé pírȉ H H H L	'whole bush'
b.	bébé kɛ̀wɛ́ H L H	bébé kɛwɛ H	bébé kɛ́wɛ̀ H H H L	'whole mon-goose'
c.	bébé sɪ́rɪ̀ H H L	bébé sɪrɪ H	bébé sɪ́rɪ̀ H H H L	'whole leopard'
d.	bébé ɓéké^ꜜké H HLH	bébé ɓekeke H	bébé ɓékékè H H H H L	'whole chin(s)'
e.	bébé kʊ́kàlɪ́ H H L H	bébé kʊkalɪ H	bébé kʊ́kálɪ̀ H H H H L	'whole fish sp.'

In (92), the second item undergoes tone change. In this case, all syllables, except the last syllable of the second item, surface with a H tone. The last syllable surfaces with a L tone. I analyze the H tone on the second item as the result of rightward spreading of the tone of the first item onto the non-final syllables of the second item. It should be noted that the L tone on the last syllable of the second item occurs irrespective of the tone melody of the first item. An explanation of the data requires the application of TD to the lexical tone melody of the non-initial item, L tone assignment to the final syllable of the second item and Rightward Tone Spread (RTS).

I propose that the same derivational steps apply to Quan + N phrases in which the initial Quan has a lexically assigned L tone, even though the surface form would be the same if one assumed rightward L tone spreading for these cases. Examples in (93) show a L-toned quantifier followed by a noun.

[24] Kalaḅarị uses a system of addition, subtraction, and multiplication in the formation of numerals above ten, and there are at least seven numeral phrase types in the lect (Jenewari 1977: 329). Also, while the numerals one, and four to ten, regularly phrase tonally with a following noun, the numeral three does not. The numeral two sometimes does not phrase with a following noun. Because of this complexity we will not consider phrases of this type in this study.

(93) Quan + N Construction

	Quan + N	TD	TM_1+L, RTS	Gloss
a.	dʒà pìrì L L	dʒà piri L	dʒà pìrì L L L	'some bushes'
b.	dʒà kɛ̀wɛ́ L L H	dʒà kɛwɛ L	dʒà kɛ̀wɛ̀ L L L	'some mon-goose'
c.	dʒà sɪ́rɪ̀ L H L	dʒà sɪrɪ L	dʒà sɪ̀rɪ̀ L L L	'some leop-ard'
d.	dʒà ɓékeꜜké L HLH	dʒà ɓekeke L	dʒà ɓèkèkè L L L L	'some chin(s)'
e.	dʒà kʊ́kàlɪ́ L H L H	dʒà kʊkalɪ L	dʒà kʊ̀kàlɪ̀ L L L L	'some fish sp.'

Let us now consider a LHL-toned quantifier followed a noun in (94) below.

(94) Quan + N

	Quan + N	TD	TM_1 +L, RTS	Gloss
a.	tɔ̃̀wã́` pìrì LHL L	tɔ̃̀wã́`piri LHL	tɔ̃̀wã́ pìrì LH L L	'many bushes'
b.	tɔ̃̀wã́` kɛ̀wɛ́ LHL L H	tɔ̃̀wã́`kɛwɛ LHL	tɔ̃̀wã́ kɛ̀wɛ̀ L H L L	'many mon-gooses'
c.	tɔ̃̀wã́` sɪ́rɪ̀ LHL H L	tɔ̃̀wã́`sɪrɪ LHL	tɔ̃̀wã́ sɪ̀rɪ̀ L H L L	'many leop-ards'
d.	tɔ̃̀wã́`ɓékéꜜké LHL HLH	tɔ̃̀wã̂ ɓekeke LHL	tɔ̃̀wã́ ɓèkèkè L H L L L	'many chins'
e.	tɔ̃̀wã́` kʊ́kàlɪ́ LHL H L H	tɔ̃̀wã́`kʊkalɪ LHL	tɔ̃̀wã́ kʊ̀kàlɪ̀ L H L LL	'many fish sp.'

A similar analysis would be proposed for the examples in (93) above which show nouns following the quantifier **tɔ̃̀wã̂**, an item with what I propose as a lexically assigned LHL tone melody. In so doing, I can also present evidence for the proposal that in this item, in addition to LH tone pattern that surfaces, there is a floating L tone. Given the deletion of the lexical tone melody of the second item in the TP, one would expect that if the underlying melody for **tɔ̃̀wã̂** were LH, it is H tone which would appear on the first syllable of the second item in (94a-c), and on the second syllable as well in (94d-e). The fact that it is L tone that appears suggests the need to posit a final floating L tone. Given the prevalence of downstepped H tone in the tone patterns of Kalaḅarị, we know that floating L tones are a normal feature of the language. Again, I propose a L tone assigned to the final syllable of the second item. The floating L tone of the LHL tone melody of the first item associates with the first syllable of the second item and in (94d-e), spreads onto the second syllable.

In order to account for the entire class of Quan + N phrases, both tone spreading and the independently occurring L tone on the last syllable of the second item have to be proposed. The latter, though not necessary to explain the examples in (93) and (94), involving as they do a L tone as the last tone on the first item, is necessary for those in (92) where the last tone on the first item is H tone. Since the proposed existence of a L tone on the final syllable of the second item does not distort the reality of the examples in (93) and (94), I propose that it applies across all Quan + N examples, irrespective of whether or not the last tone of a Quan is L tone, as in (93) and (94).

In all this, the crucial generalization that falls out from the analysis is that the L tone on the final syllable of the TP is assigned by the morphological class of the first item, which in each case is a quantifier. It will become increasingly evident in the sections below that any tone melody in the TP additional to that lexically associated with the first item is always determined by the morphological class of the first item.

Further, the proposal in (94) requires the presence in the second item, of a L tone owing its origin to the spread of the last tone of the lexical melody of the first item. It requires also that this be immediately adjacent to a L tone assigned to the final syllable of the second item by the morphological class of the first item. This appears to violate the OCP which states that no adjacent identical melodies should occur within a representation. This violation, however, is apparent rather than real. OCP was originally intended to apply to tones assigned within the lexical domain and, by extension, tones assigned within a single level of the phonology. The tones which apparently violate OCP in Kalaḅarị are tones which are (i) generated by the lexical domain and spreading in the phrasal phonology as a result of TD, and (ii) tones appearing in the phrasal domain generated by the morphological class of the first item, i.e. the identical adjacent tones are supplied by the two different domains of the phonology, one lexical, the other, assigned by the morphological class. One L tone is part of the lexical specification of the first item, and the other of specification by its morphological class. In addition, whereas the former is assigned directly to the lexical item, the second is assigned to the second item in these TPs. Since the OCP is constrained to operate at a single level only, two identical adjacent tones, one lexical, the other specified by morphological class, one associated with the word, the other with the phrase, do not represent OCP violation.

3.3.3 Tone Phrases with H Tone Melody

H-toned phrasal constructions involve two types of syntactic constructions in Kalaḅarị. These are demonstrative + Noun (Dem + N) and Interrogative + Noun (Int + N) Constructions.

A H tone occurs in Demonstrative + Noun constructions (Dem + N). There are five demonstratives in Kalaḅarị, as listed in (95) below.

(95) a. má 'this' (feminine singular)
b. ɓí 'this' (masculine singular)
c. mí 'this' (neuter singular)
d. má 'these' (plural)
e. míꜜná 'these' (plural)

Historically, (95e) is a compound item deriving from **mí** 'this' and **íná** 'their'. In contexts in which **míꜜná**[25] occurs, **má** (95d) may be substituted without changing the meaning of the construction. However, **má** is mostly restricted to contexts in which the speaker expresses some disgust (Jenewari (cf. 1977). As in the determiner system, the plural forms, **má** and **míꜜná**, are neutral to gender. The illustrations in (96) show demonstrative plus noun constructions.

(96) Dem + N

	Dem + N	TD	TM_1 + H, RTS	Gloss
a.	mî pìrì HL L	mí ` piri HL	mí pìrí H L H	'this bush'
b.	mî námá HL H	mí ` nama HL	mí nàmá H L H	'this animal'
c.	ɓí ` kɛ̀wɛ́ HL L H	ɓí ` kɛwɛ HL	ɓí kɛ̀wɛ́ H L H	'this mongoose'
d.	ɓí ` sɪ́rɪ̀ HL H L	ɓí ` sɪrɪ HL	ɓí sɪ̀rɪ́ H L H	'this leopard'
e.	má ` ɓékéꜜké HL HLH	má ` ɓekeke HL	má ɓèkèké H L L H	'these chins'
f.	má ` kʊ́kàlɪ́ HL H L H	má ` kʊkalɪ HL	má kʊ̀kàlɪ́ H L L H	'these fish sp.'

I propose that the monosyllabic demonstratives above have a lexically assigned HL melody. The justification for this can now be given. As we have already noted, as is the pattern in Kalaḅarị, all tone melodies associated with non-initial items are deleted in a TP. The last tone of the first item is what spreads onto the following items. Here, in (96), instead of surface H spreading, as occurred in (86b) where H tone was the last tone of the first item, we see L appearing on the first syllable of the second item and in (96e) spreading onto the second syllable. This suggests that, as in the case of **tɔ̀wâ**, there is a floating final L tone which gets associated with the syllables of the following item in the TP, and then spreads onto any following non-final syllable, as can be seen particularly in (96e-f). Further spread is blocked by the presence of the H tone on the rightmost syllable of the non-initial item, as seen in the examples above. This H tone on the rightmost syllable of the second item is the product of the morphological class of demonstrative to which the head of the TP belongs.

Moving on to interrogative + noun constructions, there are four interrogative modifiers, listed in (97).

---

25 This may also be historically a complex of three morphemes mi-ni-a (Williamson, p.c.)

(97) a. tɔ̀ 'what, which'
b. tʊ̀ɓɔ́ 'who, whose'
c. ǹdâɪ 'how much, many'
d. ǹdɛ́ꜜɛ́ 'what, which'

The examples involving interrogative modifiers given in (98) below and elsewhere in this study will involve the use of **tɔ̀**. The other three modifiers at times behave tonally like **tɔ̀** in relation to the following nouns, but at other times they form a separate TP from the constituents they precede. Historically, these forms were polymorphemic and this may explain their tendency to sometimes behave like independent tone phrases.

(98) Int + N

	Int + N	TD	TM_1 + H, RTS	Gloss
a.	tɔ̀ pìrì L L	tɔ̀ piri L	tɔ̀ pìrí L LH	'which bush?'
b.	tɔ̀ námá L H	tɔ̀ nama L	tɔ̀ nàmá L L H	'which meat?'
c.	tɔ̀ kɛ̀wɛ́ L LH	tɔ̀ kɛwɛ L	tɔ̀ kɛ̀wɛ́ L LH	'which mongoose?'
d.	tɔ̀ sɪ́rɪ̀ L HL	tɔ̀ sɪrɪ L	tɔ̀ sɪ̀rɪ́ L LH	'which leopard?'
e.	tɔ̀ ɓékèꜜké L HLH	tɔ̀ ɓekeke L	tɔ̀ ɓèkèké L L LH	'which chin?'
f.	tɔ̀ kʊ́kàlɪ́ L HLH	tɔ̀ kʊkalɪ L	tɔ̀ kʊ̀kàlɪ́ L LLH	'which fish sp.?'

From the forms in (98) we see that the last syllable of the second item surfaces with a H tone. Any syllable preceding the last linked syllable has a L tone by rightward L tone spread from the first item. I propose here also that the H tone melody which occurs independently of the lexical tone of the first item links onto the rightmost syllable of the second item in the phrase in the two-item TPs. This H tone melody is entirely predictable from the morphological class of the first item, here interrogative.

3.3.4 Tone Phrases with HL Tone Melody

Four types of constructions occur with HL melody. These are, namely, modifying Verb + Noun (V + N), Noun + Noun (N +N), possessive pronoun + Noun with the /ɓɔ/ (Pro + N-ɓɔ) and Noun-object + V (N-Obj + V) constructions. Both classes of initial items, noun and verb, produce the same tonal effect. I will demonstrate here with L-toned initial noun in such constructions, in (99).

(99) Initial item with L Tone Melody

	V + N	TD	TM_1+HL, RTS	Gloss
a.	ɗɛ̀rì pȉrȉ L L	ɗɛ̀rì piri L	ɗɛ̀rì píȉ L L H L	'laughing bush'
b.	ɗɛ̀rì kʊ́kàlí L H L H	ɗɛ̀rì kʊkalı L	ɗɛ̀rì kʊ̀káɫ̀ı L L L H L	'laughing fish'
	N + N			
c.	fìnì pȉrȉ L L	fìnì piri L	fìnì píȉ L L H L	'fire bush'
d.	fìnì kʊ́kàɫ́ı L H L H	fìnì kʊkalı HL	fìnì kʊ̀káɫ̀ı L L L H L	'fire fish sp.'
	N-object + V			
e.	ɓùrù kpó↓pú L HLH	ɓùrù kpopu L	ɓùrù kpópù L L H L	lit. yam hold 'hold yam'
f.	ɓùrù kpɔ́kìrí L H L H	ɓùrù kpɔkırı L	ɓùrù kpɔ̀kírì L L L H L	lit. yam pick 'pick yam'
	Pro + N-ɓɔ́ + N			
g.	̀ınà ɗàɓɔ́ L L H	̀ınà ɗaɓɔ L	̀ınà ɗáɓɔ̀ L L H L	'their father-person'
h.	̀ınà ǰìŋgiɓɔ́ L L H	̀ınà jiŋgiɓɔ L	̀ınà ǰìŋgíɓɔ̀ LL L H L	'their mother-person'

In the forms in (99), the second item is reduced in column 3 with a HL tone pattern, occurring on the last two syllables. In (99b), (99d), (99f) and (99h) the L tone on the first syllable of the second item is as a result of the L tone spreading from the first item. To account for the HL tones on the final syllables of the second item, I propose that they constitute a HL melody which is assigned by the morphological class of the first items.

Let us consider further examples in (100) below showing phrases with a HL-toned initial item. There are no possessive pronouns with a HL melody.

(100) Initial Item with HL Tone Melody

	V + N	TD	TM_1 + HL, RTS	Gloss
a.	wúrà pìrì HL L	wúrà piri HL	wúrà pírì H L H L	'hastening bush'
b.	wúrà kʊ́kàlɪ́ HL H L H	wúrà kʊkalɪ HL	wúrà kʊ̀kálɪ̂ H L L H L	'hastening fish'
	N + N			
c.	gógò pìrì HL L	gógò piri HL	gógò pírì H L H L	Gogo's bush'
d.	gógò kʊ́kàlɪ́ HL H L H	gógò kʊkalɪ HL	gógò kʊ̀kálɪ̂ H L LH L	'Gogo's fish sp.'
	N-object + V			
e.	ɪ́kù dɛ̀rɪ̀ HL L	ɪ́kù dɛrɪ HL	ɪ́kù dɛ́rɪ̀ H L H L	lit. cocoyam sell 'sell cocoyam'
f.	ɪ́kù kpɔ́kɪ̀rɪ́ H L H L H	ɪ́kù kpɔkɪrɪ HL	ɪ́kù kpɔ̀kɪ́rɪ̀ H L LH L	lit. cocoyam yam 'pick cocoyam'

From the forms in (100), we observe that in column 3 the tone on the last two syllables of the second item appears as a HL melody. In the initial syllable of the second item of (100b), (100d) and (100f) a preceding L tone occurs. This preceding L tone may be analyzed as a result of the L tone spreading from the first item (cf. (99) also). The evidence suggests that the HL tones on the last two syllables constitute a tone melody assigned by the morphological class of the first item.

We will now consider, in (101) below, data in which a H-toned initial item occurs in the TP.

(101) Initial Item with H Tone Melody

	V + N	TD	TM_1+HL, RTS	Gloss
a.	ɓɔ́rɔ́ pìrì H L	ɓɔ́rɔ́ piri H	ɓɔ́rɔ́ pírì H H HL	'passing bush'
b.	ɓɔ́rɔ́ kʊ́kàlɪ́ H H L H	ɓɔ́rɔ́ kʊkalɪ H	ɓɔ́rɔ́ kʊ́káɪ̂ H H H HL	'passing fish'
	N + N			
c.	kásá pìrì H L	kásá piri H	kásá pírì H H H L	'rack bush'
d.	kásá kʊ́kàlɪ́ H H L H	kásá kʊkalɪ H	kásá kʊ́káɪ̂ H H H HL	'rack fish'
	Pro + N-ɓɔ			
e.	á ɗà ɓɔ̀ H L L	á ɗa ɓɔ H	á ɗá ɓɔ̀ H H L	'her father-person'
f.	í jìngì ɓɔ̀ H L L	í jiŋgi ɓɔ H	í jíngíɓɔ̀ H H H L	'your mother-person'
	N-object+ V			
g.	námá dɛ̀rɪ̀ H L	námá dɛrɪ H	námá dɛ́rɪ̀ H H H L	lit. meat sell 'sell meat'
h.	námá kpɔ́kɪ̀rɪ́ H H L H	námá kpɔkɪrɪ H	námá kpɔ́kɪ́rɪ̀ H H H HL	lit. meat pick 'pick meat'

The tone of the second item in the forms is also reduced and a HL tone pattern appears on the last two syllables. Given the examples in (101), the HL tones on the last two syllables would seem to constitute a tone melody assigned by the morphological class of the first item. In the case of (101b), (101d), (101f) and (101h) the H tone on the initial syllable of the second item is as a result of rightward spreading of the H tone from the first item. The analysis is consistent with the proposal that, in Kalaḅarị, the HL melody is assigned by the morphological class of the first items.

Again, we see an apparent OCP violation, this time involving the spread H tone of (101b), (101d), (101f) and (101h) immediately adjacent to the H tone of the HL melody assigned by the morphological class of the first item. However, the data in (100) establish that the HL melody on the last two syllables of the second item exists independently of the tone melody of the first item. In addition, as I argue in relation to phrases beginning with Quan, the two adjacent identical tones are generated by two different sources, one lexical, the other marking morphological class and appearing on the surface via the operation of quite distinct rules. There is thus arguably no real OCP violation.

Jenewari (1977: 99) cites an exceptional situation where both the modifier and the following noun undergo tone change. The modifiers that are nouns in this case have HLH and LH melodies, respectively, and the data stated there belong to tone phrase constructions bounded by HL melody. In this case, the underlying tone melodies of the modifiers are optionally reduced to HL, while the head nouns receive the HL melody assigned by the T-head in some cases. The data taken from (Jenewari 1977: 99) are illustrated in (102) below.

(102) a. ɠòɠə́ wáꜜrí → [ɠòɠə́ wárì] ~ [ɠòɠò wárì]
Gogo house 'Gogo's house'

b. ópùró kànà → [ópùró káná] ~ [ópùrò kàná]
shrimps basket 'basket of (or for) shrimps'

c. ékùlé wáꜜrí → [ékùlé wárí] ~ [ékùlè wàrí]
kite house 'kite's house'

As can be seen above, the H tone of the modifier optionally reduces to a L tone. In (102a), the reduction of the tone on the T-head does not affect the expected result on the following noun. However, in (102b) and (102c) the expected HL does not surface rather the high of the modifier spreads unto all the following syllables or spreads to the first syllable only. Although, Jenewari cites two options only for (102b) and (102c), native speakers do produce additional two acceptable forms, as shown below.

(103)a. ópùró kànà → [ópùró kánà] ~ [ópùrò kánà]
shrimps basket 'basket of (or for) shrimps'

b. ékùlé wáꜜrí → [ékùlé wárì] ~ [ékùlè wárì]
kite house 'kite's house'

Like in (102a), the examples above show that the phrasal HL may appear on non-initial items despite the change on the T-head within the phrase. I cannot explain the tone change on the T-head at this point, but the fact remains that these exceptional cases belong to tone phrases bounded by HL melody, as the data in (102) and (103) illustrate. The T-head tone change as noted by Jenewari will constitute a part of wider Kalaḅarị tonal study to come.

3.3.5 Tone Phrases with HLH Tone Melody

We may distinguish two types of constructions in which a HLH melody occurs. These are possessive pronoun + noun constructions which express non-intimate possessive relationships and those that contain distal demonstratives preceding the noun.

3.3.5.1 Non-Intimate Possessive Pronoun + Noun

In constructions of this type the noun immediately following the possessive pronoun is never a noun expressing close affinal or intimate relationship, in contrast with possessed nouns **ɟ̃ìŋgì** 'mother', **ɗà** 'father', **tà** 'wife' and **ɗì** 'husband' which are discussed in §3.3.1 above. The examples given in (104) show possessive pronouns which vary between a V and VCV structure, depending on whether the following noun begins with a vowel or a consonant, as discussed in §1.4.1.1.

(104) Pro + N

	Pro + N	TD	TM$_1$+HLH, RTS	Gloss
a.	ɪ̀nà pɪ̀rɪ̀ L L	ɪ̀nà piri L	ɪ̀nà pí꜌rí L L HLH	'their bush'
b.	ɪ̀nà námá L H	ɪ̀nà nama L	ɪ̀nà ná꜌má L L H L H	'their animal'
c.	ɔ̀ kɛwɛ́ L L H	ɔ̀ kɛwɛ L	ɔ̀ kɛ́꜌wɛ́ L H L H	'his mon-goose'
d.	á sɪ́rɪ̀ H H L	á sɪrɪ H	á sɪ́꜌rɪ́ H HLH	'her leop-ard'
e.	wánà ɓéké꜌ké HL HLH	wánà ɓekeke HL	wánà ɓèké꜌ké H L · L HLH	'our chins'
f.	wánà kʊ́kàlɪ́ HL H L H	wánà kʊkalɪ HL	wánà kʊ̀ká꜌lɪ́ H L L HLH	'our fish sp.'

The forms in (104) show that the second items all surface with HLH tone melodies with the L floating between the two H tones. The initial L tone on the second item in (104e-f) is as the result of L tone spreading from the possessive pronoun. I propose that the tones on the last two syllables in the second item constitute HLH tone melody assigned by the morphological class of the initial item. We presume that, given the fact that the other melodies associated with morphological class are L, H and HL, the HLH melody is a combination of HL and H rather than of H and LH.

As demonstrated so far, possessive pronouns have three different possible effects on TPs within which they occur as the initial items. Firstly, no tone melody appears if the noun in the possessive construction refers to close kin relationship such as father, mother and wife, as discussed in §3.3.2. In the second type, a HL melody occurs if the kinship noun is followed by ɓɔ́, as discussed in §3.3.4. In the third type, a HL and H melodies appear on the following noun, as discussed in §3.3.5.1. We noted that the possessed nouns of the third type are nouns not included in the first and second types. Given that the possessive pronoun is the initial item, in all these types of phrases the leftmost item or tonological head alone cannot account for the difference in the occurrence or non-occurrence of tone melodies in these constructions.

The presence or absence of a tone melody and the identity of the melody in these cases is clearly determined by the semantic class of the phrase. As we know already, in the possessive constructions in which no tone melody appears, the noun is a kinship term referring to a close or intimate affineal relationship. In the cases where the possessed noun appears with a ɓɔ, a HL tone melody appears. In the non-intimate possessed constructions, in which HL and H appear, the HL and H mark non-intimate possessive relationships. The tonal differences in these constructions signal these semantic differences in otherwise identical syntactic structural types.

The difference in behavior between intimate possession and non-intimate possession is not unknown in African linguistics. Such a distinction has earlier been proposed to account for structural differences in possessive constructions in African languages such as Bongo and Mamvu (Claudi and Heine 1989) and references cited there. For example, Claudi and Heine (1989: 8) propose that:

> in Mamvu the structure without a genitive linker is confined to the expression of 'more intimate' relations, while the linker ɓà occurs with 'less intimate' ones.

They give the following data, presented in (105) below supporting their proposal.

(105) a. mu - mgódo 'my daughter'
b. mu - garú 'my foot'
c. ini - ɓà qínga 'your (sg.) bicycle'

The forms in (105a) and (105b) indicate intimate possession by way of the absence of an overt linker. By contrast, in (105c), the presence of the linker **ɓà** marks the construction as a non-intimate possessive.

Although the examples given in the Mamvu data do not involve tonal differences, there is some parallel between the Mamvu data and tonal processes in pronominal possessive constructions in Kalaḅarị. The parallel in Kalaḅarị is that an intimate pronominal possessive construction shows no tone melody attributable to the morphological class of the initial item, while a non-intimate possessive construction does via HL and H melodies.

3.3.5.2 Distal Demonstrative + Noun

A distal demonstrative (DD) construction expresses a degree of relative distance from the speaker (Jenewari 1977: 253-255). Such a phrase contains a distal demonstrative modifier as the initial item and a noun as the head. The following are items used as modifiers in this class.

(106) a. àǹì 'that, those'
b. ó꜌sí 'other'

To illustrate, I use examples showing **àǹì** followed by a noun. The glosses in (107) indicate that DD + N constructions can have at least two interpretations.

(107) DD + N

	DD + N	TD	TM_1 +HLH, RTS	Gloss
a.	ànì pìrì L L	ànì piri L	ànì pí↓rí L L HLH	a. 'that bush' b. 'its bush'
b.	ànì námá L H	ànì nama L	ànì ná↓má L L H L H	a. 'that animal' b. 'its animal'
c.	ànì kɛ̀wɛ́ L L H	ànì kɛwɛ L	ànì kɛ́↓wɛ́ L L H L H	'that mongoose' b. 'its mongoose'
d.	ànì sɪ́rɪ̀ L H L	ànì sɪrɪ L	ànì sɪ́↓rɪ́ L L HLH	a. 'that leopard' b. 'its leopard'
e.	ànì ɓéké↓ké L HLH	ànì ɓekeke L	ànì ɓèké↓ké L L LH LH	a. 'that chin' b. 'its chin'
f.	ànì kʊ́kàlɪ́ L H L H	ànì kʊkalɪ L	ànì kʊ̀ká↓lɪ́ L L L HLH	a. 'that fish sp.' b. 'its fish sp.'

From the data in (107) we again see that the second item surfaces with a HLH tone pattern on its last two syllables. Non-distal demonstratives, as we noted in our discussion of the examples in (90)-(91) assign a H tone to the last syllable of the second item. Why, one might ask, do distal demonstratives behave so differently? The answer may lie in the fact that the **ànì**-phrase is capable of two interpretations; **ànì** as a possessive pronoun or as a DD. If we assume that **ànì** is being treated tonally as a possessive pronoun in spite of its actual interpretation in the construction, then the tone patterns exhibited in (107) are properly accounted for, since they share the characteristics of a non-intimate possessive pronoun + N construction by having a HLH melody. Thus such distal demonstratives have the same tonal effects on the TP as non-intimate possessive pronouns with which they share the same form. Demonstratives assign H tone to the second item when they do not have forms interpretable as possessive pronouns.

3.4 Tone Processes in Sequences Larger Than Two Items

In this section, the tone patterns in structures that are three- and four-word sequences will be discussed. Evidence from TPs involving two items cannot tell us whether tone melodies assigned to the end of the non-initial item by the morphological class of the initial item are being assigned to (i) the second item or (ii) the final item of the TP. Longer sequences will help us decide.

3.4.1 Three and Four-word Sequences with L Tone Melody

As we have already seen, simple quantifier plus noun (Quan + N) constructions have a L tone assigned by the morphological class of the first item. Let us look at what happens when a quantifier precedes two or three nouns in a construction. The examples in (108) below show a H-toned quantifier preceding two nouns. The glosses give two possible meanings for these sequences. In each case, the a. gloss reflects the possible treatment of the N + N sequence, where Quan modifies this N + N, whereas the b. gloss reflects the possible treatment of the first N as the possessor of the following N, with Quan modifying the initial N. As can be seen here, this syntactic difference has no consequence for the surface tone pattern.

(108) Q + N_1 + N_2 Sequence

	Quan + N_1 + N_2	TD	TM_1 + L, RTS
a.	bébé pìrì kíꜜrí H L HLH	bébé piri kiri H	bébé pírì kìrì H H H L LL a. 'whole bush ground' b. 'whole bush's ground'
b.	bébé námá kíꜜrí H H HLH	bébé nama kiri H	bébé námà kìrì H H H L L L a. 'whole meat ground' b. 'whole meat('s) ground'
c.	bébé kɛ̀wɛ́ kíꜜrí H LH HLH	bébé kɛwɛ kiri H	bébé kɛ́wɛ̀ kìrì H H H L L L a. 'whole mongoose ground' b. 'whole mongoose's ground'
d.	bébé sɪ́rɪ̀ kíꜜrí H H L HLH	bébé sɪrɪ kiri H	bébé sɪ́rɪ̀ kìrì H H H L L L a. 'whole leopard ground' b. 'whole leopard's ground'
e.	bébé kʊ́kàlɪ́ kíꜜrí H HLH HLH	bébé kʊkalɪ kiri H	bébé kʊ́kálɪ̀ kìrì H H H H L L L a. 'whole fish(sp.) ground' b. 'whole fish's (sp.) ground'

From the examples in (108) above, with H-toned initial quantifiers, we see that after tone reduction on the non-initial items a L tone is assigned to the last syllable of the second item in the TP. The H tone on the initial item spreads onto the first syllable of the second item. The assigned L tone then spreads rightwards onto the following item. The examples in (108) suggest that the L tone originating in the morphological class of the Quan T-head is assigned to the final syllable of the second item.

The examples in (108) for the first time provide evidence that the L tone melody assigned by the quantifier is not assigned to a syntactic boundary. In the b. interpretation of Q + N_1 + N_2 sequences, Q + N_1 forms a syntactic constituent, N', but in the a. interpretation Q + N_1 does not form a syntactic constituent. Syntactic parsing for the (a) interpretation would by N_1 + N_2 forms $[_{NP}$ [Q] $[_{N'}$ [N_1]] N_2] and for the (b) one, Q + N_1 form a possessor of N_2: $[_{NP}$ $[_{N'}$ [Q N_1]] N_2].

If the assigned L tone marked a syntactic domain, we would have expected a L tone to be assigned to the final syllable of the third item, N_2, in the (a) cases. Instead, the L tone in both interpretations is assigned to N_1, the second item in the construction. This suggests that even though the TP in Kalaḅarị corresponds to syntactic phrases, NP and VP, the internal branching of these phrases is irrelevant to the assignment of this L tone.

Constructions such as those in (109) below, in which the initial quantifier itself has a lexically assigned L tone, can fit into the analysis proposed for the location of L tone generated by Quan. However, they cannot shed any additional support for this analysis.

(109) Q+ N_1 + N_2 Sequence

	Q+ N_1 + N_2	TD	TM_1 + L , RTS
a.	dʒà pȉrȉ kí꜡rí L L HLH	dʒà piri kiri L	dʒà pȉrȉ kȉrȉ L L L̓ L L a. 'some bush ground' b. 'some bush's ground'
b.	dʒà námá kí꜡rí L H HLH	dʒà nama kiri L	dʒà nàmà kȉrȉ L L L L L a. 'some animal ground' b. 'some animal's ground'

In (110) below, we will briefly consider a four-word sequence. As in (108-109), there are two possible interpretations. In each case, the a. gloss reflects the possible treatment of the N + N + N sequence, where Quan modifies this N + N + N, whereas the b. gloss reflects the possible treatment of the second N as the possessor of the following N, with the quantifier modifying the initial N.

(110) $Q + N_1 + N_2 + N_3$ Sequence

$Q + N_1 + N_2 + N_3$	TD	TM_1 + L, RTS
bébé pìrì féní wáꜜrí H L H HLH	bébé piri feni warı H	bébé pírì fènì wàrì H H H L L L L L a. 'whole bush bird nest' b. 'whole bush bird's nest'

This four-word sequence confirms that the L tone assigned by the morphological class of the initial item is indeed assigned to the second item rather than to the penultimate or final item of the phrase. It also confirms that the assignment of this tone is blind to the internal structure of the syntactic phrase to which the TP corresponds.

The rule in (111) formalizes the association of the L tone determined by the morphological class of the initial item. M represents the morphological class of the initial word, while 'W' represents the non-initial word.

(111) L-Association

[[M] $[_W (C_1V)$ CVCV]...$]_{TP}$

T* L

Condition: M = quantifier
T* = any tone melody

The derivation in (112) below shows the application of this rule in addition to TD and RTS rules in the derivation of the Quan + N construction, **bébé kánákánà** 'whole darkness'.

(112) be be + kana kana — Lexical Association
H H

[be be ka nakana] — TD
H

[be be kanakana] — L Association
H L

[be be kanakana] — RTS
H L

[bébé kánákánà] — Output

3.4.2 Three and Four-word Sequences with H Tone Melody

Simple interrogative plus noun (Int + N) and demonstrative plus noun (Dem + N) constructions have a H tone assigned to the final syllable of the noun. Here, we want to consider what happens when the Int or Dem precedes two or three nouns. Let us consider the data in (113) below, in which the interrogative precedes two nouns. As in (108), (109) and (110), there are two possible interpretations of such constructions; one in which $N_1 + N_2$ is modified by Int (the a. glosses) and one in which Int + N_1 modify N_2 (the b. glosses). The syntactic bracketing would be as follows, $[_{NP}[\text{Int}]\ [_{N'}\ [N_1\ ]]\ N_2]$ for the (a) gloss and $[_{NP}\ [_{N'}\ [\text{Int}\ N_1]]\ N_2]$ for the (b).

(113) Int + N_1 + N_2 Sequence

	Int + N_1 + N_2	TD	TM_1 + H, RTS
a.	tɔ̀ pìrì wáꜜrɪ́ L L HLH	tɔ̀ piri warɪ L	tɔ̀ pìrì wàrɪ́ L L L L H a. 'which bush house?' b. 'which bush's house?'
b.	tɔ̀ námá wáꜜrɪ́ L H HLH	tɔ̀ nama warɪ L	tɔ̀ nàmà wàrɪ́ L L L L H a. 'which meat house?' b. 'which meat's house?'
c.	tɔ̀ kɛ̀wɛ́ wáꜜrɪ́ L L H HLH	tɔ̀ kɛwɛ warɪ L	tɔ̀ kɛ̀wɛ̀ wàrɪ́ L L L L H a. 'which mongoose house?' b. 'which mongoose's house?'
d.	tɔ̀ sɪ́rɪ̀ wáꜜrɪ́ L H L HLH	tɔ̀ sɪrɪ warɪ L	tɔ̀ sɪ̀rɪ̀ wàrɪ́ L L L L H a. 'which leopard house?' b. 'which leopard's house?'
e.	tɔ̀ kʊ́kàlɪ́ wáꜜrɪ́ L HLH HLH	tɔ̀ kʊkalɪ warɪ L	tɔ̀ kʊ̀kàlɪ̀ wàrɪ́ L L L L L H a. 'which fish house? b. 'which fish's house?'

From the forms in (113) we see that all syllables except the last surface with a L tone. The identical tones are as a result of the rightward spreading of the lexically assigned L tone of the interrogative. The last syllable of the rightmost item in the phrase surfaces with a H tone.

Consider also the examples in (114) below in which a demonstrative precedes two nouns. As in the data above, the glosses also have two possible interpretations, depending on whether they are parsed as; a. $N_1 + N_2$ modified by Dem forms $[_{NP}\ [\ \text{Det}]\ [_{N'}\ [N_1\ ]]\ N_2\ ]$ or as b. Det + N_1 as a possessor of N_2 or $[_{NP}\ [_{N'}\ [\text{Dem}\ N_1]]\ N_2]$.'

(114) Dem + N_1 + N_2 Sequence

	Dem + N_1 + N_2	TD	TM_1 + H, RTS
a.	mí` pȉrì kíꜜrî HL L HLH	mî piri kiri HL	mí pȉrì kȉrí H LL L H a. 'this bush ground' b.'this bush's ground'
b.	mi^ féní kíꜜrí HL H HLH	mî feni kiri HL	mí fènȉ kȉrǐ H L L L H a. 'this bird ground' b. 'this bird's ground'
c.	mi^ kɛ̀wɛ́ kíꜜrí HL L H HLH	mí` kɛwɛ kiri HL	mí kɛ̀wɛ̀ kȉrí H L L L H a. 'this mongoose ground' b. 'this mon-goose's ground'
d.	mi^ sírì kíꜜrí HL HL HLH	mi^ sɪrɪ kiri HL	mí sȉrì kȉrí H LL L H a. 'this leopard ground' b. 'this leopard's ground'
e.	mi^ kʊ́kàlí kíꜜrí HL HLH HLH	mí` kʊkalɪ kiri HL	mí kʊ̀kàlȉ kȉrí H L L L L H a. 'this fish (sp.) ground' b. 'this fish's (sp.) ground'

From the forms in (114), as in (113), we see that all syllables in the non-initial items, except the last in the TP, surface with a L tone, which is derivable from rightward spread of the last lexically assigned tone of the initial item. The last syllable of the rightmost item surfaces with a H tone. The examples in (114) seem to confirm that the H tone associated with Int and Dem is assigned to the last syllable of the rightmost item.

This applies even when Int or Dem modifiers precede three nouns, irrespective of the internal syntactic structure of the TP, as in (115) below. There are also two possible interpretations in this case. The a. gloss reflects the possible treatment of the N + N + N sequence, where Int/Dem modifies this N + N + N, whereas the b. gloss reflects the possible treatment of the second N as the possessor of the following N, with Int/Dem modifying the initial N.

(115) Int/Dem + N_1 + N_2 + N_3 Sequence

	Int + N_1 + N_2 +N_3	Tone Deletion	TM_1 + H, RTS
a.	tɔ̀ pìrì féní wáꜜrí L L H HLH	tɔ̀ piri feni warı L	tɔ̀ pìrì fènì wàrí L LL LL LH a. 'which bush bird nest?' b. 'which bush bird's nest?'
b.	mı^ pìrì féní wáꜜrí HL L H HLH	mí ` piri feni warı HL	mí pìrì fènì wàrí H LLLL LH a. 'this bush bird nest' b. 'this bush bird's nest'

In (116) below, I propose a rule which assigns the H tone associated with Int and Dem to the final syllable of the last item in the TP.

(116) H Association

```
[[M]  [W1 (C1V) CVCV]...[W2 (C1V) CVCV] ]TP
  |                                   |         Condition:
  T*                                  H         M = Dem, Int
```

(117) below shows the application of this rule in addition to TD and RTS rules in the derivation of the Int + N construction, **tɔ̀ ɓèkèké** 'which chin?'

(117) tɔ + ɓekeke — Lexical Association
L HL H

[tɔ + ɓekeke] — TD
L

[tɔ ɓekeke] — H Association
L H

[tɔ ɓekeke] — RTS
L H

[tɔ̀ ɓèkèké] — Output

3.4.3 Three and Four-word Sequences with HL Tone Melody

We have seen that simple N + N and N + V constructions have HL melody assigned by the morphological class of the initial item. Here we will consider what happens when the modifying N precedes two and three-word sequences in a phrase. The examples that follow in (118) below are constructions in which an initial noun precedes a noun and a verb. Such phrases are VP constructions which have an internal N-object followed by a verb. The syntactic structure of these TPs is $[_{VP} [_{V'} [_{NP} [N_1 N_2]] V]]$.

(118) $N_1 + N_2 + V$ Sequence

	$N_1 + N_2 + V$	TD	TM_1 + HL, RTS
a.	pi̋ri̋ fını̀ pɛ́lɛ́ L L H	pi̋ri̋ fını pɛlɛ L	pi̋ri̋ fínı̀ pɛ̀lɛ̀ L L HL L L 'to cut bush firewood'
b.	pi̋ri̋ námá pɛ́lɛ́ L H H	pi̋ri̋ nama pɛlɛ L	pi̋ri̋ námà pɛ̀lɛ̀ L L H L L L 'to cut bush animal'
c.	pi̋ri̋ kɛ̀wɛ́ pɛ́lɛ L H H	pi̋ri̋ kɛwɛ pɛlɛ L	pi̋ri̋ kɛ́wɛ̀ pɛ̀lɛ̀ L L H L L L 'to cut bush mongoose'
d.	pi̋ri̋ sírı̀ pɛ́lɛ́ L HL H	pi̋ri̋ siri pɛlɛ L	pi̋ri̋ sírı̀ pɛ̀lɛ̀ LL H L L L 'to cut bush leopard'
e.	pi̋ri̋ kʊ́kàlí pɛ́lɛ́ L L HLH H	pi̋ri̋ kʊkalı pɛlɛ L	pi̋ri̋ kʊ̀káli̋ pɛ̀lɛ̀ LL L H L L L 'to cut bush fish (sp.)'

The data in (118) indicate that the HL melody associated with the morphological class of the initial item is assigned to the last two syllables of the second item rather than the final item of the TP. The data showing $N_1 + N_2 + N_3$ sequences in (119) and $N_1 + N_2 + N_3 + N_4$ sequences in (120) confirm this.

(119) $N_1 + N_2 + N_3$ Sequence

	$N_1 + N_2 + N_3$	TD	TM_1 + HL, RTS
a.	pȉrȉ fɪnɪ̀ kíꜜrí L L HLH	pȉrȉ fɪnɪ kiri L	pȉrȉ fɪ́nɪ̀ kȉrȉ L LH LL L a. 'bush firewood ground' b. 'bush fire's ground'
b.	pȉrȉ námá kíꜜrî L H HLH	pȉrȉ nama kiri L	pȉrȉ námà kȉrȉ L L H L L L a. 'bush animal ground' b. 'bush animal's ground'
c.	pȉrȉ kɛ̀wɛ́ kíꜜrí L L H HLH	pȉrȉ kɛwɛ kiri L	pȉrȉ kɛ́wɛ̀ kȉrȉ LL H L L L a. 'bush mongoose ground' b. 'bush mon-goose's ground'
d.	pȉrȉ sɪ́rɪ̀ kíꜜrí L HL HLH	pȉrȉ sɪrɪ kiri L	pȉrȉ sɪ́rɪ̀ kȉrȉ LL HL L L a. 'bush leopard ground' b. 'bush leopard's ground'
e.	pȉrȉ kʊ́kàlɪ́ kíꜜrí L L HLH HLH	pȉrȉ kʊkalɪ kiri L	pȉrȉ kʊ̀kálȉ kȉrȉ LL H L L L L a. 'bush fish (sp.) ground' b. 'bush fish's (sp.) ground'

(120) $N_1 + N_2 + N_3 + V/N_4$ Sequence

	$N_1 + N_2$ $+N_3$ $+V$	TD	TM_1 + HL, RTS
a.	pìrì féní wáꜜrí pɛ́lɛ́ L H HLH H	piri feni warı pɛlɛ L	pìrì fénì wàrì pɛ̀lɛ̀ L L H L L L L L a. 'to cut bush bird nest' b. to cut bush bird's nest
	$N_1 + N_2$ $+N_3$ $+N_4$		
b.	pìrì féní wáꜜrí kíꜜrí L H HLH HLH	pìrì feni warı kiri L	pìrì fénì wàrì kìrì L L H L L L L L a. 'bush bird nest ground' b. 'bush bird's nest ground'

(121) provides the rule which assigns the HL melody determined by the morphological class of the initial item in constructions headed by nouns and verbs. The melody is assigned to the last two syllables of the second item, associating the tones and the syllables in a R→L direction.

(121) HL Association Rule

```
[[M]         [W1(C1V)CVCV]...]TP
  |                  |  |              Condition:
  T*                 H  L              M = N, V
```

(122) below shows the application of this rule in addition to TD and RTS rules in the derivation of the N + N construction, **pìrì kòkáìì** 'bush fish'.

```
(122)   pi ri   + kʊkalɪ        Lexical Association
        \/        | | |
        L         H LH

        [piri   kʊkalɪ]         TD
         \/
         L

        [pi ri  kʊkalɪ]         HL Association
         \/        : :
         L         H L

        [piri   kʊkalɪ]         RTS
         \/.......  | |
         L          H L

        [pìrì kʊ̀kálɪ̂]           Output
```

3.4.4 Three and Four-word Sequences with HL and H Melodies

I next examine assignment of the HL and H tone melodies marking non-intimate possessive pronoun + noun constructions, previously dealt within two-item TPs in §3.3.5. With these constructions, there are two possible interpretations as well, one in which $N_1 + N_2$ is modified by the possessor, the a. glosses, and one in which Pro + N_1 modify N_2, the b. glosses. Again, different possible syntactic analyses are not reflected in differences in the surface tone patterns.

(123) Pro + N_1 + N_2 Sequence

	Pro + N_1 +N_2	TD	TM_1 + HL, H, RTS
a.	ɪ̀nà fɪ̀nɪ̀ kíꜜrí̂ L L HLH	ɪ̀nà fɪnɪkiri L	ɪ̀nà fɪ̀nɪ́ kìrí L L LH L H a. 'their firewood ground' b. 'their fire's ground'
b.	ɪ̀nà námá kíꜜrî L H HLH	ɪ̀nà nama kiri L	ɪ̀nà nàmá kìrí L L L H L H a. 'their animal ground' b. 'their animal's ground'
c.	ɪ̀nà kɛ̀wɛ́ kíꜜrí L L H HLH	ɪ̀nà kɛwɛ kiri L	ɪ̀nà kɛ̀wɛ́ kìrí L L L H L H a. 'their mongoose ground' b. 'their mongoose's ground'
d.	ɪ̀nà sɪ́rɪ̀ kíꜜrí L HL HLH	ɪ̀nà sɪrɪ kiri L	ɪ̀nà sɪ̀rɪ́ kìrî LL LH L H a. 'their leopard ground' b. 'their leopard's ground'
e.	ɪ̀nà kíꜜrí kʊ́kàlɪ́ L HLH HLH	ɪ̀nà kiri kʊkakɪ L	ɪ̀nà kìrí kʊ̀kàlɪ́ L L LH L L H a. 'their ground fish (sp.)' b. 'their ground's fish (sp.)'

As the forms in (123) show, the first H tone in the HL melody is assigned to the last syllable of the second item, whereas the L tone is assigned to the first syllable of the third item. Also, the second H is assigned to the last syllable of the third item. The rightward spreading of the lexical L tone of the initial item accounts for the identical L tones on following syllables.

In four-word sequences in (124) below, we see that the H of the HL tone melody is assigned to the final syllable of the second item, and the H tone melody to the last syllable of the fourth item with the intermediate syllables bearing L tone. Since the H tone melody is appearing on the third item in three-word TPs and on the fourth item in four-word TPs, it is clear that it is being assigned to the item occupying the TP boundary.

(124) Pro + N_2 + N_3 + N_4 Sequence

	Pro + N_2 + N_3 + N_4	TD	TM_1 + HL, H, RTS
a.	ɪ̀nà pìrì féní wá↓rí L L H HLH	ɪ̀nà piri feni warı L	ɪ̀nà pìrí fènì wàrí L L LH L L LH 'their bush bird('s) nest?'
b.	o pìrì féní wá↓rí L	ò piri feni warı L	ò pìrí fènì wàrí L LH L L L H 'his bush bird('s) nest'

The problem is now one of explaining why the initial H tone of the HL melody appears on the final syllable of the second item, whereas the remaining H tone appears on the last syllable of the final item.

In the preceding sections, we have seen two different patterns for the assignment of the melody assigned by the initial item to following items in three-word and four-word sequences: (i) the melody is assigned to the final syllable of the final item in the sequence. This was seen to apply where the sequence consists of Int/Dem + N_1 (+ N_2 + N_3); intermediate syllables then received tone by rightward spreading of the final tone of the lexically assigned melody of the initial item. (ii) The melody is assigned to the final syllable(s) of the second item in the sequence. Any following toneless syllables then receive tone by rightward spreading of the final tone of the melody assigned by the morphological class of initial item. This was seen to apply to sequences of Quan + N_1 (+ N_2 + N_3), N_1 (+ N_2 + N_3) +V, and N_1 + N_2 (+ N_3 + N_4).

The data in (123) and (124) show that there is yet a third possibility, in which the HL and H melodies of the possessive pronoun in a non-intimate possessive construction are seemingly split over the second and third item, the final syllable of second item receiving the initial HL melody, the remaining H melody appearing on the final item.

In the TPs examined in §3.4.3, L of the HL melody appears on the final syllable of the second item. On the other hand, the forms in (123) and (124) show the L tone appearing on the first syllable of the third item in the sequence. Non-intimate possessive pronouns thus produce two melodies, HL, and the H melody on the last syllable of the final item in the TP.

Although in (123) and (124) we can account for the association of the H tone melody, the manner of the association of the initial HL melody constitutes a problem for my proposal. On the one hand, the HL melody shares an association with the second item with the HL melody on TPs in which verbs and nominals are the initial items. However, while the HL is assigned to the two last syllables of the item for the examples in (120) via R→L association, it is the H of the HL melody which is assigned to the final syllable in that position in the cases in (123) and (124), i.e. possessive pronoun plus noun constructions.

I propose that non-intimate possessive pronoun marks the last syllable of the immediately following item in the syntactic construction by an extra unspecified word-final HL, which is the tone melody assigned to the last two syllables of the second item in all TPs begun by the overall class of nominals which include possessive pronouns, then gets associated following the normal R→L association in Kalaḅarị. The inserted V syllable, however, triggers V deletion rule which deletes the inserted V, delinking the assigned L tone. The L tone is either left floating as in two-word sequences or reassigned to the initial syllable of an immediately following item in sequences longer than two words. I propose a V-insertion rule in (125) below.

(125) V-Insertion (Non-intimate Possessive Pronouns)[26]
Insert a second V_2 after the rightmost V_1 in the second word in a non-intimate possessive construction

```
                    V
                    ↓              Condition: TP = Non-intimate
[[M] [W1(C1V) CV - ]...]TP         M = Possessive pronoun
```

I give a derivation of ɪ̀nà kʊ̀ká↓lɪ́, 'their fish (sp.)', in (126) below in which the V-Insertion, H, HL assignments, V-deletion and RTS apply.

```
(126)  ɪna  kʊkalɪ              Lexical Association
       \/    | | |
       L     H LH

       [ɪna  kʊkalɪ]            TD
       \/
       L

       [ɪna   kʊ kalɪɪ]         V-insertion
       \/
       L

       [ɪna  kʊ kalɪ ɪ]         HL, H Association
       \/        : : :
       L         H LH

       [ɪna   k ʊ kalɪ ɪ]       RTS
       \/......      | | |
       L             H LH

       [ɪna  kʊkal ɪ]           V-deletion
       \//         | |
       L          HLH

       [ɪ̀nà kʊ̀ká↓lɪ́]            Output
```

I give further derivation of three-word sequences in (127) below which shows the application of the rules mentioned above. The example is **ɪ̀nà pòló sʊ̀kʊ̀lʊ́** 'their compound's school'.

---

[26] Williamson (p.c.) suggests a rule of tone shift one syllable to the right. Possible evidence can be found in other KOIN lects such as Iḅanị and Nkọrọọ.

(127) ɪna polo sukulu — Lexical Association
L H L H L

[ɪna po lo sukulu] — TD
L

[ɪna po loo sukulu] — V-insertion
L

[ɪna poloo sukulu] — HL, H Association
L HL H

[ɪna poloo sukulu] — RTS
L HL H

[ɪna polo sukulu] — V-deletion/L-association
L H L H

[ɪ̀nà pòló sùkùlú] — Output

3.5 Summary

The tonal analysis of phrasal constructions yields so far the result that the left-most item or the T-head in the phrase plays a significant role in determining the surface pattern of the tone phrase. This item is the only one to preserve its underlying lexical tone. The surface tone of the rest of the TP is at least partly accounted for by reference to this melody. However, in addition, there are tonal effects in the TP which cannot be so accounted for. These additional effects come from the morphological class of the initial item.

In addition, we have seen that NP and VP constitute domains for tone phrasing. In these domains, the morphological specifications and, in a subcategory, the semantic specifications of the initial items determine the tone melody which is assigned to either the second item or the final item, or distributed over these in the TP. The H melody determined by non-distal Dem/Int and possessive pronouns in non-intimate possessive constructions is assigned to the last item in the sequence. The L tone determined by quantifiers and the HL melody determined by modifying nouns and possessive pronouns in non-intimate constructions are assigned to the immediately following item rather than the final item. The HL melody in non-intimate possessive constructions is the melody associated with a nominal T-head (noun and possessive pronoun), and the final H melody is the one used for non-distal demonstratives.

The presence of HL melody in non-intimate possessive pronoun constructions is explained by the fact that possessive pronouns belong to the category of nominals. On the other hand, possessive pronouns behave like Dem in that they both assign a H melody to the final syllable of the rightmost item in the TP. The relationship between possessive pronouns and demonstratives may be explained by the fact that they form part of the same number and gender system in Kalaḅarị, hence the same distinctions show up at the tonal level.

Besides the positions mentioned above, association of these melodies proceeds linearly without further regard to syntactic ranking or bar level. Given the linearity of association, tone phrasing suggests a left-headed and a right-branching prosodic structure in which the initial item determines the tone of the immediately following items. Although the domain of the TP is syntactically determined, the prosodic structure that is built in that domain is independent of its syntactic structure which is right-headed and left-branching. Assuming a binary branching structure, the left-branching structure in (128) below represents the syntactic structure of Kalaḅarị. S represents the head of the structure.

(128) Right-headed, Left-Branching Structure

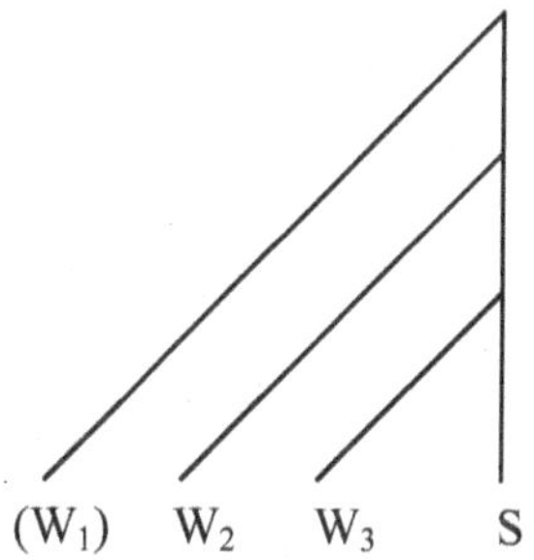

On the other hand the left-headed, right-branching structure (129) below represents the prosodic structure of Kalaḅarị. In the prosodic structure the initial item is the head.

(129) Left- headed, Right-branching Prosodic Structure

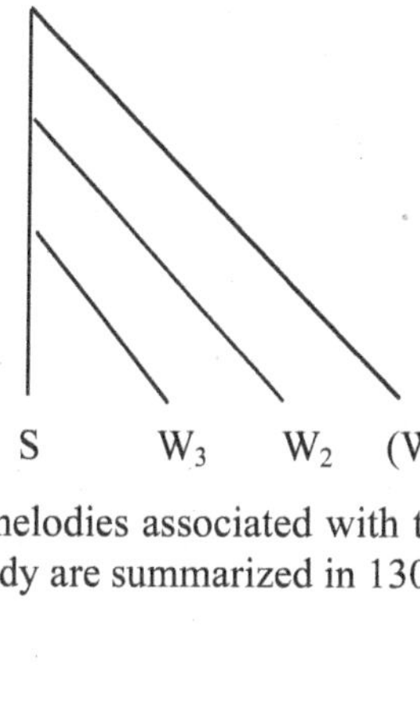

The melodies associated with the different phrasal constructions considered in this study are summarized in 130 below.

(130) Morphological/Semantically Determined Tone Melodies

	Morph Class of Initial item/Semantic Category	Tone Melody
a.	Lexical Modifier	
	i. V/N + N	HL
	ii. N-object + V	HL
b.	Possessive Pronoun Modifier	
	i. Intimate poss + N	none
	ii. Intimate poss + N-ɓɔ	HL
	iii. Non-intimate poss + N	HL & H
c.	Non-nominal Modifier	
	i. Quan + N	L
	ii. Non-distal Dem/Int + N	H

4

Syntactic Domains of Tone Phrase

4.0 Introduction

In the previous chapter, we were careful not to specify all the syntactic domains that corresponded to the tone phrase. We are now able to deal with this issue in some detail.

4.1 Syntactic Phrases in which TD Applies

We have seen in Chapter 3 that TD applies to delete the lexically assigned tone melody of the non-initial elements. The TD rule proposed to account for tone deletion in these domains is repeated in (131) below.

(131) Tone Deletion Rule (TD)
In a tone phrase (TP), all words in a non-initial position delete their tone.

$[[W_1]\ [W_2] \dots [W_N]]_{TP}$

```
  |     |         |
  T*    T*        T*
        ↓         ↓
        Ø         Ø
```

W = Word
T* = any tone melody

We considered in detail the six phrase types in which TD applies, as given in the summary in (132) below. These phrases constitute subtypes of the NP and VP domains within which TD operates.

(132) a. NP
- i. having an initial pronominal possessor
- ii. having an initial interrogative demonstrative
- iii. having a demonstrative
- iv. having an initial quantifier
- v. having a noun, be it a possessor or the first member of a compound (N + N).

b. VP
Obj-NP + V

Crucially, TD predicts that the lexical tone melody of every non-initial item, including the syntactic head, must be deleted in the domain in Kalaḅarị. However, in the following, we will see that not every syntactic head deletes its lexically assigned tone melody in the domain.

4.2 Syntactic Phrases in which TD does not Apply

In the following, we will examine the phrase types that do not undergo tone changes. (133) lists the major phrase types in which the TD does not apply.

(133) a. [$_{DP}$ [NP] D]

b. [$_{IP}$ [NP] $_{I'}$[VP] I]

The following are examples of the major phrases in which TD does not apply. Note that the earlier examples of NP and VP in Chapter 3 show that one would expect the tone determined by the morphological class of the initial item which is assigned to the second item to spread to the third item. However, here the determiner following the NP retains its lexically assigned tone melody, as seen in (134) below.

(134) a. /pìrì námá mɛ́ / → [$_{DP}$ [$_{NP}$ pìrì námà] mɛ́]
L H H → LL HL H
bush animal the — 'the bush animal'

b. /ìndʒì kàngàrá mɛ́/ → [$_{DP}$ [$_{NP}$ ìndʒì kàŋgárá] mɛ́]
L LH H → L L LHL H
fish rack the — 'the fish rack'

As can be seen here, the determiner, which is post nominal, is not tonally affected.

Similarly, in the IP (135) a tense-aspect-negation marker,[27] henceforth TAN, which follows the verb in Kalaḅarị, retains its lexically assigned tone melody. It is useful to note that ASP and NEG do not co-occur in Kalaḅarị.

[27] Jenewari (1977: 440-560) provides some details of the T/A/N distinctions of Kalaḅarị.

(135)

a. [pìrì námá][gògó ɓá] árì → [IP [NPpìrì námà][VP [NP gògó]ɓá] árì]
L H LH H HL LL HL LH H HL
S O V INFL
bush animal Gogo kill ASP '(a) bush animal (is) killing Gogo'

b. [gògó tùɓɔ̀][ɪnà tùɓɔ̀ fòmù] [á'á]→
LH L L L L HLH
S O V INFL

Gogo child their child beat NEG

[IP [NP gògó túɓɔ̀] [VP [NP ɪ̀nà tú'ɓɔ́] V fómú] á'á]
LH HL LL HLH HH HLH
'Gogo's child did not beat their child'

In the examples above, the TAN markers surface with either HL or HL and H melodies. These are their underlying tone melodies.

Further, in a VP in which the NP is followed by a determiner, the determiner retains its lexically assigned tone melody, but the lexically assigned tone melody of the verb is deleted. The verb receives the tone of the determiner by rightward tone spreading, as in the example given below.

(136) [gògó tùɓɔ̀ ɓé] fòmù] → [vp [DP [NP [gògó túɓɔ̀] ɓé] fómú]
LH L H L LH H L H HH
Noun Noun Det V
Gogo child the beat 'beat (the) Gogo's Child'

As can be seen above, the underlying tone melody of the verb is deleted, allowing the H tone on the determiner to spread rightwards onto the verb. The verb is not part of the DP, but forms a tone phrase with the preceding determiner in the DP. This is a further example which shows that tone phrasing does not always correspond to syntactic phrasing.

4.3 Tone Deletion Rule (Revised)

From the above, it has been established that TD operates within NP and VP, but not in DP and IP. The difference between these is that the former have lexical heads, i.e. nouns and verbs, whereas the latter have functional heads, i.e. Dets and TANs. To reflect this fact, I propose a revision of the tone deletion rule in (137) below.

(137) Tone Deletion Rule (Revised)
Every non-initial item in a phrase headed by a lexical category deletes its tone relative to the item to its left provided that the item is not itself a functional head.

[[W$_1$] [W$_2$]...[$_{head}$ W]]$_{XP}$
| | |
T* T* T*
↓ ↓ W = Functional head
Ø ØT* = Tone melody

A tone phrase can therefore be defined as being made up of either (i) an NP or (ii) a VP, which ever is the higher constituent. This latter proviso accommodates the phrasing of Obj-NP with a VP, as in the examples below.

(138)

a. /pìrì námá dóꜜkí/ → [$_{VP}$ [$_{V'}$[$_{NP}$pìrì námà] dòkì]]
L H HLH — L L H L L L
bush animal carry — 'carry bush animal'
N N V

b. /ɓʊ̀rʊ̀ árì féní wáꜜrí/ → [$_{NP}$ [$_{IP}$ [$_{VP}$ ɓʊ̀rʊ̀]árì] fènì wàrì]
L HL H HLH — L L H L L L L L
rot ASP bird house — 'rotting bird's house'

Similarly, we can account for tonal behavior of serial verb constructions (SVC) in Kalaḅarị in which the lexically assigned tone melodies on the verbs occurring in series are maintained. This suggests the verbs in such a construction do not form a single tone phrase. Before we look at the problems such constructions have for the theory proposed here, let us consider the examples in (139). The subject is omitted since we already know that a subject constitutes a tone phrase separately from the VP.

(139) a. /ɪnà nàŋgá sáɓá/ → [ɪnà nàŋgà][sáɓá]
L L H H — L L L L H H
them trample cross — 'cross them by trampling'

b. /tɛ́ꜜkɛ́ gògó pìrì/ → [tɛ́ꜜkɛ́] [gògó pírí]
H LH L H L — HL H L H H H
pray gogo give — 'pray for Gogo'

c. /màŋgɪ̀ sáɓá / → [màŋgɪ̀] [sáɓá]
L H — L L H H
run cross — 'run across'

In the examples (139a) and (139b) it is clear that the object, if present, forms a TP with the immediately following verb. This verb deletes its lexically assigned tone melody and takes on the tone of the object. It is also clear that the two verbs of a SVC do not phrase together even where no object is present, as (139c) shows. The tone of the initial verb does not affect the following verb. Given the tone-phrasing algorithm in (137), verbs in serial constructions belong to separate TPs. If there is indeed a correspondence between TPs and maximal projections, this would imply that serial verbs occupy separate maximal structures.

Constructions given in (139), which may be considered single syntactic units, are behaving tonally as separate units. Why are such cases not forming single tone phrases in which TD applies? Two possibilities exist. Either (i) these are not syntactically single units or (ii) there is not a one to one correspondence between syntactic phrase and tone phrase. The first of these options, I think, best accounts for these two types of constructions.

In the case of serialization, languages make use of two types of serial constructions. These are coordinating and subordinating serial verb constructions. Sebba (1987) addresses the question of whether serialization is a coordinating or subordinating structure in languages. If we assume a subordinating representation in Kalaḅarị we cannot explain why tone on the second verb is not deleted in (139), since the verb must be a part of the VP. On the other hand, if we assume a coordinating syntactic structure, the second verb would clearly constitute a separate VP and TD would not apply. This latter is what the tonal evidence suggests occurs in Kalaḅarị. In support of this, we should note that the examples in (139) can optionally take the conjunction marker **tɛ́** 'and' as shown in (140) below.

		→	
(140) a.	/ˋɪnà nàŋgá tɛ́ sáɓá/	→	[[ˋɪnà nàŋgà] [tɛ́] [sáɓá]]
	L LH H H		L L L L H H H
	them trample and cross		'trample and cross them'
b.	/tɛ́ꜜkɛ́ tɛ́ gògó pɪ̀rɪ̀/	→	[[tɛ́ꜜkɛ́] [tɛ́][gògó pɪ́rɪ́]]
	HLH H L H L		HLH H L H H H
	pray and gogo give		'pray for Gogo'
c.	/màŋgɪ̀ tɛ́ sáɓá/	→	[[màŋgɪ̀] [tɛ́] [sáɓá]]
	L H H		L L H H H
	run and cross		'run and cross'

From the data in (140) we can see that serial verbs constructions with the conjunction marker **tɛ́** are like conjoined NPs in Kalaḅarị. This along with the tonal evidence suggests that the conjoining version of serialization is the one applicable in Kalaḅarị.

4.4 Summary

With the proposals given above, we are able to explain the following:

(i) TD fails to apply in the IP and DP, which are the maximal projections of the functional heads, I, D.

(ii) TD applies within NP, VP, which are the maximal projections of the lexical heads, N, V.

The (ii) forms TPs, although the prosodic structure deriving from the left-branching syntactic domains is actually right-branching, as discussed in Chapter 3.

5

Conclusions

5.0 Introduction

In this study, I have presented a detailed account of aspects of the complex tonal system of Kalaḅarị. The complexity is found at both the lexical and phrasal levels of the phonology. I was able to explain the complexity at both levels by drawing attention to the effects other levels of the grammar have on tone association in Kalaḅarị.

5.1 Tone Association

Accounts of tone association in most languages assume a left-to-right convention. However, in this study, left-to-right mapping was considered and rejected. It was clearly shown that a right-to-left mapping convention provides the best account of well-formed tonal representations in Kalaḅarị. Like Hausa, Kalaḅarị is one of the growing numbers of languages in which linguists recognize that the tonal system can only be properly analyzed by proposing right-to-left association convention. My findings in relation to Kalaḅarị lexical tone association rules provide strong evidence that not all Ịjọ lects operate the usual left-to-right tone association at the lexical level, which is the general assumption among Ịjọ scholars. This suggests that some Ịjọ lects may be like Kalaḅarị, right-to-left tone mapping, in particular the East Ịjọ lects of which Kalaḅarị is a part. The implications are therefore quite obvious, i.e. the need for a systematic investigation of the pitch systems of other relatively less studied Ịjọ lects.

5.1.1 Segmental Processes and Tone Association

In Chapter 2, I proposed that Kalaḅarị tone patterns appearing on items may be distinguished into two basic types: (i) those with floating L tone and (ii) those without. I argued that a L tone floats only when it is delinked from its original V-syllable as a result of an independently motivated V-deletion rule. This analysis provided a simple account of floating L tone and also explains distinctive downstep in lexical items in Kalaḅarị. It reduces the complexity of the tonal system by showing that a floating tone does not occur as part of the underlying tonal representation of items in the lexicon. A floating L tone is as a result of the presence of a V-V sequence to which a segmental V deletion rule applies. Thus floating L tone is predictable in Kalaḅarị strictly by reference to the segmental specification of items.

From the regular application of R→L association convention, we got some insights as to how tones are assigned in loanwords from European languages. Apparent deviant surface patterns such as HLL and HHLL which occur with loan words were explained by default L tone which is assigned to vowels inserted to produce acceptable Kalaḅarị syllables. The evidence suggested that bilinguals may have as their underlying lexical representations for loans structures which violate surface Kalaḅarị segmental rules and this has an effect on surface tone realization. This reinforces the point already made about floating L tone, that apparent deviations may owe their presence to segmental processes.

5.2 Syntax and Phrase Tonology

I found, with Williamson (1988: 253-78), that the diagnostic feature for a tone phrase is a deletion rule which applies to remove any previously assigned tone on words in non-initial position. Like Williamson (1988: 253-78), I established that tone deletion occurs if the non-initial word is within the same syntactic phrase as the initial word. Thus we concluded that a tone phrase is determined by the syntactic domains, NP and VP, the only phrase types with open class lexical heads. This scenario as detailed in Williamson (1988: 253-78) is a general phenomenon found in other Ijoid languages.

Tone phrasing, however, does not always correspond to syntactic phrasing. Thus in a VP which includes DP, the NP within the DP constitutes a TP. The DP cannot since phrases headed by functional items are blocked from doing so. The sequence of Det and V, as the residue of the syntactic phrase headed by V, also form a TP though they do not constitute a syntactic phrase.

It has been proposed in the literature on syntax-phonology interface that morphological specifications of terminal elements appear not to be one of the features interacting with phonology (Inkelas and Zec 1990, 1995: 536). However, it is clearly shown that, in Kalaḅarị, the surface pitch pattern of a tone phrase is determined by both the lexical and morphological specifications of the initial item. The lexically assigned tone or the lexically assigned tone along with a tone melody assigned by the morphological class of the initial item entirely determine the surface tone pattern of the phrase.

Since lexical tone surfaces on the lexical item to which it is assigned, morphological tone has to surface on an item later in the TP that has had its lexical tone deleted by the TD rule. Kalaḅarị clearly demonstrates the effects of the morphological specification of terminal elements on phonology. An analysis which does not recognize this contribution to the pitch pattern of the phrase will fail also to recognize the important role syntax plays in the tonal phonology at the phrasal level. The contribution of morphological specifications to tone association at the phrasal level provides new evidence in favor of further morpho-syntactic interaction with phonology.

5.3 OCP and Phrase Tonology

OCP, as we have seen applies, at the lexical domain, but not at the phrasal domain in Kalaḅarị. This relates to one of the issues raised in the literature concerning OCP, whether it applies only in a non-derived domain, or it applies also in derived domains such as the word or phrase. The literature is filled with cases in which the OCP applies in both non-derived and derived domains in languages. On the other hand, languages also exist in which OCP applies in a non-derived domain, while not applying in a derived domain (Odden 1995: 461). In the version of OCP proposed in Odden (1995: 464), languages have the option of doing something about an OCP violation or doing nothing about OCP violation. As we can see in this study, Kalaḅarị has decided to adopt the second option, i.e. allowing adjacent identical tones with different derivational histories at the phrasal level. Attempting to make an analysis which avoids an OCP violation in the Kalaḅarị data simply leads to complex and unrevealing analysis of the facts of tone processes at the level of the phrasal phonology.

5.4 Concluding Remarks

This study provides the first extended in-depth study of the tonal grammar of Kalaḅarị, one of the Ijoid lects. It is hoped that it will contribute significantly to the understanding of the complex pitch patterns of Ijoid lects, some of which are considered by tonologists to be quite unusual. Also, it is hoped that this study would stimulate further investigations of related phenomena in other Ijoid and non-Ijoid tone systems.

Appendix

Introduction

The items in the tables of the following pages represent an extended dataset selected from about 3,747 items in the manuscript of the dictionary compiled by S. Owuye. The tables illustrate tone patterns in monosyllabic to quadrisyllabic items. The approximate number of forms that exist in the database for each pattern is put in brackets in the relevant sections of the tables. Each pattern is illustrated with twenty items, where possible. For each tone pattern, the items are divided into V-initial and C-initial items, respectively. The aim is to demonstrate that tone patterns occur in morphemes irrespective of their canonical shape. This division is only possible with monosyllabic, bisyllabic and trisyllabic patterns. It is not possible in quadrisyllabic patterns because of the fewer number of C-initial items in that category.

The appendix is divided into two sections. The first section lists tone patterns of native items while the second section lists tone patterns of loan words and items whose sources are questionable. The first letter of the syllabic pattern followed by a numeral is used to identify each set of data.

1. Tone Patterns of Native Items

Monosyllabic Patterns (L, H)

M1

L (200)		H (220)	
Item	Gloss	Item	Gloss
à	‘I’	á	‘she/her’
ɪ̀ ~ ì	‘my’	ɪ́~í	‘you(r)’ sg.
ɔ̀ ~ ò	‘he/his’	ɔ́ ~ ó	‘you’ pl.
sò	‘sky/heaven’	só	‘go’
sɔ̀	‘cook’	sɔ́	‘enter’
ɗà	‘father’	sá	‘debt’
dì	‘husband’	sú	‘put’
tà	‘wife’	ɓú	‘drink/smoke’
fà	‘lose’	ɓó	‘to come’
dà	‘govern/hold’	sɛ́	‘stand/nation’
sɪ̃̀	‘drink /remove’	sã́	‘urine’
bɪ̃̀	‘quench (as in fire)’	fṹ	‘dirt/refuse’
fʊ̃̀	‘blow (as in nose)’	bɪ̃́	‘pick/discover’
ɗɪ̃̀	‘understand/learn’	sṹ	‘hat’
fɪ̃̀	‘fly’	fʊ̃́	‘salt’
kɪ̃̀	‘to tap (liquid)’	kã́	‘tear (V)’
kʊ̃̀	‘catch’	dʒẽ́	‘another’
sɪ̃̀	‘call’	gbɪ̃́	‘throw/sew’
nà	‘hear’	ɗɪ̃́	‘night’
fɪ̀	‘die’	ɓɪ̃́	‘full’

Bisyllabic Patterns, LL, LH, HH, HL, HLH

B1

LL (288)		L H (178)	
Item	Gloss	Item	Gloss
àkà	'trick/technique'	èkpé	'he-goat'
òfò	'rayfish'	ìrí	'thread'
ìkè	'hunchback'	àmbá	''sister'
ɔ̀mɔ̀	'ebb'	àmʊ́	'hang'
òpù	'big/important'	àpá	'fool/ fish species'
èkpè	'chest'	òkí	'fish species'
àkʊ̀	'bee'	ìmɔ́	'to fast'
ɛ̀dɛ̀	'funeral bed'	ɔ̀fɔ́	'ceremonial stick'
ànì	'that'	èké	'shout of joy'
ìjì	'give birth'	ɛ̀kpɛ́	'tribal mark'
pòkù	'bat'	dàmá	'confront'
màngì	'run'	ɗìsɛ́	'sneeze'
mɛ̀nì	'swallow'	ɓʊ̀rá	'excess'
sànì	'pepper'	ɓìrí	'dress up'
pùlò	'oil'	fìá	'agree'
ɓèrì	'are'	gɔ̀gí	'deform'
pɔ̀kɔ̀	'throat'	sìá	'divorce'
fìnì	'fire'	gàrí	'garri'
kìkɔ̀	'scrotum'	ɗàwɔ́	'learn'
mènì	'flesh'	sàkí	'get up'

B2

HH (316)		HL[28] (180)	
Item	Gloss	Item	Gloss
ílá	'intestine'	ásʊ̀	'odor'
ádʒʊ́	'head pad'	ádʒì	'fish species'
ágbá	'paint'	íkù	'cocoyam'
ígbé	'box'	élè	'space'
éré	'female'	éwù	'an expression'
íkú	'louse'	ítì	'enlarged foot'
ókú	'message'	ífì	'kid's game'
ɛ́kí	'to slice'	ílʊ̀	'fish habitat'
ɔ́kí	'take'	óɓù	'dumb', aphesis'
íkʊ́	'stone/rock'	ɔ́gì	'gonorrhea'
ɓíɓí	'mouth'	bélè	'light'
bébé	'whole'	nínè	'eight' (num)
féní	'bird'	sírì	'leopard'
kúró	'fall'		
pókú	'bundle'		
námá	'animal/meat'		
pɔ́kʊ́	'waterside'		
píkɔ́	'feather'		
mɛ́nɛ́	'ant'		
tírá	'three		

[28]The C-initial nouns above exhaust the native items with this pattern in the database. Other items found in the database are loan words from European languages.

B3

H⁴H[29] (202)

Item	Gloss
á⁴ɗɔ́	sister-in-law
á⁴kʊ́	'bitter'
é⁴bé	'insect sp.'
é⁴né	'rain'
ɛ́⁴gɛ́	'knot/stone'
ʊ́⁴dʒʊ́	'body'
ʊ́⁴mɪ́	'the other'
í⁴wʊ́	'go up'
ɔ́⁴lɔ́	'hold'
sá⁴kí	'lift/raise'
sʊ́⁴á	'put'
tɔ́⁴rʊ́	'face'
fɪ́⁴lá	'saliva'
kí⁴rí	'ground'
lɔ́⁴kɔ́	'be soft'
dé⁴é	'drive away'
ɓá⁴rá	'hand'
fʊ́⁴rʊ́	'stomach'
gbʊ́⁴rí	'to fence'

29 In Nkọrọọ (one of the lects of KOIN), the cognate nouns are diachronically reduced to a HL pattern, while verbs retain the H⁴H pattern.

Trisyllabic Patterns: LLL, LLH, LHL, LHꜜH, HHH, HLH, HHL, HHꜜH, HꜜHH

T1

LLL[30] (220)		LLH (212)	
Item	Gloss	Item	Gloss
àbàdʒì	'ocean'	àkàlʊ́	'moon/month'
òbìrì	'dog'	ɔ̀ngɔ̀rí	'snore'
èbùbè	'glory'	òdòdó	'snake'
èbèkà	'alter'	èkìrá	'roar'
ɛ̀dɛ̀lɛ̀	'vulture'	ɔ̀mɔ̀mɔ́	'housefly'
ìgbìkì	'money'	àɓã̀ĩ́	'pus'
ɪ̀gànɪ̀	'annoy'	àgàrá	'side/part'
ògìgó	'compound'	ɛ̀gɛ̀rɛ́	'bowlegs'
ɔ̀ngʊ̀rʊ̀	'spine'	èrìsé	'storm'
ɔ̀tàdʒɪ̀	'shrub'	ìɓèré	'long ago'
dʒʊ̀rɔ̀rɔ̀	'watery'	fòngòló	'be round'
dʒʊ̀lɛ̀pʊ̀	'soggy'	ɓɛ̀kɛ̀rɛ́	'lance/pike'
kpìkìrì	'short'	gbàrɪ̀á	'miss'
kpìkpìrì	'blunt'	lòlìá	'star'
lùbùlù	'sheath'	kòɓìrí	'gather' (v.t.)
lʊ̀gbàɪ̀	'paralyse'	kʊ̀kʊ̀rá	'fish species'
sʊ̃̀ɛ̃̀ɪ̀	'sponge'	nʊ̀nʊ̀má	'elastic'
tòkùrù	'part of jaw'	pàkàmá	'relation'
vʊ̀rɔ̀rɔ̀	'flowing'	pʊ̀rʊ̀kʊ́	'ruffle'
Wɛ̀kɛ̀lɛ̀	'broad'	sòlòló	'hang up'

[30]Most of the items found in the database are V-initial items.

T2

LHL[31] (172)

Item	Gloss
àbáĺì	‘cannon’
àbárà	‘boast’
àgírì	‘masquerade type’
èpéȉ	‘thread type’
ɛ̀níà	‘son’
ìbóròo	‘fish-net type’
òkóȉ	‘drum type’
òlíì	‘a shout’
ɔ̀kíkɔ̀	‘spoon’
ɔ̀kʊ́rɔ̀	‘encirclement’
àkpáȉ	‘hat type’
àkpáĺì	‘mat’
ìkpóò	‘a somersault’
àkídì	‘beans’
ɔ̀kíkɔ̀	‘spoon’
bèbúrè	‘excl. of joy’
ɓòlíà	‘dolphin’
m̀bárà	‘sister’
wɔ̀nkírɛ̀	‘now’
sòkúù	‘name town’

LHꜜH[32] (140)

Item	Gloss
àdáꜜká	‘rashes’
àláꜜgbá	‘gun’
ìfʊ́ꜜɓá	‘cassava’
ɔ̀ɓɔ́ꜜkɔ́	‘chicken’
ı̀ngbúꜜá	‘seed type’
ı̀ngéꜜlé[33]	‘metal gong’
ı̀nkéꜜlú	‘kingfisher’
òɓúꜜtú	‘shade’
òtóꜜló	‘pit/pond’
ɔ̀kɔ́ꜜkɔ́	‘skull’
ı̀mgbúꜜɓá	‘seed type’
àláꜜpá	‘fish sp.’
èréꜜké	‘tops’
ògbóꜜó	‘charm word’
òlóꜜí	‘nutritious’
ɔ̀mɔ́mꜜbɔ́	‘sand-fly’
ɔ̀tíꜜrí	‘tree sp.’
gı̀lóꜜlí	‘lure’
sı̀káꜜká	‘kapok’
pèlíꜜá	‘lady-fish’

[31] The database confirms Jenewari (1980: 23) claim that only nouns and loan words occur with this pattern. The last five items in seem to be the only native C-initial nouns in the language.
[32] C-initial items in this pattern are highly restricted.
[33] This can be pronounced as ı̀ngélè. This also the expected form in Nkọrọọ, which reduces nouns with (L)HLH pattern to (L)HL.

T3

HHH (260)		HHL (222)	
Item	Gloss	Item	Gloss
ákpákpá	'shell'	énémè	'oil palm'
íkákí	'tortoise'	ábúbà	'egg shell'
ákʊ́á	'drum/trouble'	áfánà	'co-wife'
ékélí	'deform'	ɔ́fíngɔ̀	'mussel'
ékpéní	'bribery'	ámbálì	'grasp firmly'
ɛ́bírí	'smart'	ánkísì	'length'
íɓúɓú	'fish species'	ɛ́wɛ́lɛ̀	'fish sp.'
ímpɔ́rí	'beard'	ídʒírè	'ant sp.
óɓórí	'goat'	íkɔ́lì	'water crab'
ɔ́ɓɔ́kʊ́	'covenant'	íkpápʊ̀	'pen-knife'
bánáná	'shine'	gbésímè	'silent'
dʊ́ɛ́í	'corpse/ghost'	bádámà	'talkative'
fúkúrú	'hole/hollow'	fúkúmà	'fish-trap'
gánáná	'bright'	gbírérè	'straight'
gbárʊ́rʊ́	'narrow'	kpʊ́kpʊ́nʊ̀	'clean/scrape'
sámʊ́nɔ́	'dry'	mímímà	'embarrass'
kʊ́kʊ́rʊ́	'small/narrow'	tʊ́ɓárà	'antelope'
pémbéré	'afloat'	tʊ́kʊ́mà	'straighten'
túɓóní	'traders'	wásámà	'scatter'
ɓúrúmá	'indigo'	wɛ́rárì	'static verb'

T4

HLH (162)

Item	Gloss
ákìó	'friend'
íɓùlú	'grey hair'
íkàrí	'thorn'
ékùlé	'kite'
édímà	'occult'
ímbùkú	'painted mussel'
íngbɔ̀kʊ́	'crimson red'
ópùró	'shrimps'
ɔ́pɔ̀lí	'gun powder'
óɗòkó	'sea snail'
kúkùlú	'balls'
Kʊ́kàlí	'fruit'
Tíbìlí	'mudfish'
Sírìtá	'praying mantis'
Tíngìlí	'roll'
wásàrá	'overflow'
wóngìrí	'stir'
Fɛ́fɛ̀rɛ́	'drag'
gbágìrí	'fry'
ókìkó	'bravo'

HHꜜH (140)

Item	Gloss
ámóꜜsú	'vampire'
ánáꜜná	'roast'
ɛ́tɛ́ꜜrɛ́	'mat'
ífíꜜkó	'foam'
ísáꜜká	'eyelash'
íjáꜜjá	'mouth sore'
óɗóꜜkó	'bite/tear'
ísúꜜké	'fur'
ólóꜜkú	'shout'
ɔ́fíꜜrí	'hot'
ɓáráꜜɓú	'electric fish'
ɓékéꜜké	'chin'
ɗúkúꜜnó	'stern'
gʊ́rɔ́ꜜrɔ́	'scrape'
kámgbúꜜló	'crab sp.'
kóróꜜmá	'put down'
míɔ́ꜜkʊ́	'now'
sákíꜜlɛ́	'so that'
sáláꜜmá	'separate'
pɛ́lɛ́ꜜmá	'bypass'

T5

HꜜHH[34] (3)

Item	Gloss
áɗꜜʊ́á	'defense'
íꜜrʊ́á	'sun'
ínꜜgóló	'limpet'

[34]These are the only nouns found in the database with this pattern. As can be seen, they are of the V-initial type. The corresponding forms for (2) and (3) in Nkọrọọ and Ịbanị are órúrá and íngòló, respectively. Similarly, in Nkọrọọ, only nouns of V-initial pattern are found with this tone pattern (cf. Harry, 1987: 60). Further, as observed by Jenewari (1980), verbs with this pattern are intransitive counterparts of their corresponding transitive verbs. This suggests that HꜜHH on such intransitive verbs are derived (grammatical) tones and not lexical. Hence, I omitted them in the dataset. This fact and the lack of tonal correspondence in these items across KOIN suggest a very complex derivational history for items with this pattern.

Quadrisyllabic Patterns: LLLL, LLLH, LLHL, LHLH, HHHH, HHLH, HLHL, HLHꜜH, HHHL and LLHꜜH

Q1

LLLL (130)

Item	Gloss
àkpàtàkà	‘divination ladder’
àmi̍ni̍gbò	‘croaker’
àtàɓìlà	‘tilapia’
àwàkìɓà	‘iguana’
i̍gùrùbè	‘locust’
i̍kèrèrè	‘small herring’
i̍tùrùmà	‘boat rear’
ìmbìràkà	‘cassava meal’
òkòlòfà	‘fish sp.’
ɔ̀pɔ̀kʊ̀rʊ̀	‘narrow pathway’
àkongòɓà	‘firefly’
ìngʊ̀ngʊ̀à	‘spring water’
ɔ̀dìdʊ̀rɔ̀	‘rope/twine’
`olòbi̍ri̍	‘pool’
ɔ̀kɔ̀lɔ̀bì	‘parrot’
ɔ̀kɔ̀sɔ̀ṛɔ̀	‘crumbs’
jàkàjàkà	‘rough’
i̍ɓòɓòɓà	‘rash/swelling’
ɔ̀ɓʊ̀kɔ̀rɔ̀	‘beetle’
gbùrògbùrò	‘mighty/great’

LLLH (100)

Item	Gloss
àgbàkùrú	‘bucket’
i̍kèlèmá	‘round’
àkpàràkpá	‘mat’
àwàràwá	‘pepper’
èwùrèwú	‘yam sp.’
èlèkèdí	‘quart bottle’
ɔ̀kpʊ̀rʊkpʊ́	‘palm fruit’
òfùràmá	‘swell’
ɔ̀pʊ̀rɔ̀pɔ́	‘fat’
ɔ̀pɔ̀pɔ̀lí	‘boil’ N.
àndàlìmá	‘bend’
àngìrìmá	‘struggle’
gàlàgàlá	‘scatter’
ɓi̍ri̍ɓi̍rí	‘early’
dàkàdàká	‘itch’
àkpʊ̀rʊ̀ká	‘thread’
màmbìrìmá	‘elude’

Q2

LLHL (6)

Item	Gloss
èdʒìmínà	‘ram’
kʊ̀rɔ̀kɔ́ndʒì	‘proud’
àpkàráwɔ̀	‘adult’

LHLH (14)

Item	Gloss
òlómìní	‘lime’
àkírìmá	‘game of tops’
òbórìbó	‘sweet potato’
ɔ̀kpɔ́rʊ̀kpɔ́	‘desmodium’
àdʒíɓùlú	‘hat type’
kɔ̀kʊ́kpɔ̀kʊ́	‘fish sp.’
làkálùkú	‘small meal’

Q3

HHHH (60)

Item	Gloss
ábílálá	‘paper’
ágbágárá	‘wood sp.’
ɛ́fɛ́rɛ́fɛ́	‘fish scales’
ígbéɓírí	‘hoop of cask’
ákáwáí	‘hard wood’
íkíríkó	‘drum’
óbóngóró	‘turtle’
ókóróɓá	‘tilapia sp.’
ótókóló	‘ladder’
ɔ́fírímá	‘shark’
ógílóló	‘puddle’
sínísíní	‘frenzy’
kánákáná	‘darkness’
gárágárá	‘smart’
ɓáláfámá	‘ferocious’
kúrúkúrú	‘black’
lókólókó	‘heartless’
sárágbálá	‘insect sp.’
jóríjórí	‘sparkle’
kɛ́mɛ́mɛ́mɛ́	‘stealth’

HHLH (16)

Item	Gloss
ófógòró	‘empty’
ékpékèré	‘sandfish’

Q4

HLHL (18)

Item	Gloss
ɓ́kìríngà	‘harmattan’
ábìnía̍à	‘mudfish’
élèlíà	‘fish sp.’
ábònía̍à	‘fish sp.’
ábɔ̀ítà	‘female tortoise’
lɔ́kòlɔ́kò	‘haste/hurry’

HLH↓H (8)

Item	Gloss
ɔ́ɓùlɔ́n↓gɔ́	‘bird sp.’
ɔ́kòrɔ́n↓gɔ́	‘croaker’

Q5

HHHL (10)

Item	Gloss
íkúlélè	‘iron’
élékímà	‘sign/example’

LLH↓H (8)

Item	Gloss
òɓùkú↓lɔ́[35]	‘back’
ɔ̀ɓʊ̀dʒʊ́↓ʊ́	‘back’
ètèlá↓á	‘road’

2. Items from Non-Native Lexicon

Kalaḅarị has had some influence from three major languages,[36] namely; Igbo, Portuguese and English. Igbo is a Niger-Congo language spoken in Eastern Nigeria, while Portuguese and English are of Indo-European origin. Igbo influence[37] came through trade and intermarriage (mainly between Kalaḅarị men and Igbo women). On the other hand, Portuguese influence came about through trade between Kalaḅarị and Portuguese merchants from the mid 15th century and English from late 17th century. English influence came through two possible sources, firstly, directly through English Christian missionaries and merchants who replaced the Portuguese and secondly, indirectly through Nigerian Pidgin English (Jones 1963: 11-20).

The lists below illustrate the items which come from the languages mentioned above. Some of these items, especially those of Portuguese origin have been completely integrated into the native lexicon, as the tone patterns show. This is confirmed by native speakers’ judgment in which they consistently identified Portuguese items as Kalaḅarị words and at the same time pointing out

[35] Items 1 and 2 appear to be derived items in the language. They are possible derivations from the lexical items, ɔ̀ɓʊ̀ ‘back’, dʒʊ ‘side’ and the empty morpheme kulo. This analysis is open to further consideration.

[36] There was Dutch contact with Kalaḅarị between early and mid 17th century (Jones 1963: 33). However, to the best of my knowledge, there is no evidence of their influence in the Kalaḅarị lexicon.

[37] Dike (1956: 30) reports that the Igbos ‘…bequeathed their language to Bonny [Ịḅanị], Okrika…. and to a certain extent influenced the language and institutions of Old and New Calabar [Kalaḅarị].’

words which are of Igbo and English origin. Most of the deviant tone patterns found in the language are those associated with items from the last two languages.

2.L1

English cognates

Item	Gloss
ámbɪ̀lálɪ̀	'umbrella'
bɪ́ꜜsɔ́pʊ̀	'bishop'
gólù	'gold/goal'
báíbʊ̀lʊ̀	'bible'
báfʊ̀	'basin'
bìlángìdì	'silky cloth'
bɪ̀rɪ́dʒɪ̀	'bridge'
bígʊ̀lʊ̀	'bugle'
'bɪ̀lédɪ̀	'blade'
bìlànkɛ́tì	'blanket'
dɛ́bìlɛ̀	'table'
dɛ́kì	'deck'
fʊ̀rɔ́kɔ̀	'frock'
gádìnì	'garden'
gɪ̀rétà	'grater'
ɔ́kʊ̀rʊ̀	'okra'
pánì	'plate'
pɛ́nsʊ̀lʊ̀	'pencil'
sɪ̀létɪ̀	'slate'
sɪ̀lɪ́ꜜpásɪ̀	'slippers'
síndʒìlì	'scissors'
sùkúlù	'school'
vɛ́lɪ́ꜜvɛ́tì	'velvet'

Portuguese cognates

Item	Gloss
áfàláfà	'cotton'
àlìpákà	'alpaca'
àrʊ̀sʊ̃́ʊ̃̀	'rice'
válà	'sail' N.
kùrúsù	'cannon'
ópùrópò	'pig'

2.L2

Igbo cognates

Item	Gloss
àɓɔ̀lɔ̀	'seed sp.'
àdá́	'first daughter'
àgʊ̀rʊ̀	'bitter liquid'
ágʊ́àkà	'gabon viper'
ɔ́kpárá	'first son'
ɔ̀lʊ́	'second child'
éků́	'soup spoon'
ìngàdʒí	'spoon'
ázízà	'broom'
ébɪ́nsɪ̀	'porcupine'
édʒɪ̀	'snail'
ɪ́nkòrò	'tom-tom'
ɔ́tàrà	'cassava meal'
ɪ́nkpú	'ant hill'
ímkpárá	'walking stick'
ɪ́nté	'trap'
ɔ̀sɪ́ꜜsá	'cockroach'

Miscellaneous

Item	Gloss
àgɪ̀dɪ́	'corn meal'
àkàrà	'bean cake'
àkɔ́tɔ́	'small container'
ábɪ̀lɪ̀	'draughts'
égèlègè	'wrestling'
ègʊ́sɪ́	'melon'
élèlándà	'orange'
ɛ́bɛ̀rɛ̀	'small tucks'
ɪ́kpɔ́ꜜkpɔ́	'fish sp.'
ɪ́ndʒɪ̀rɪ̀	'cloth type'

References

Akinlabi, A. 1995. ATR-harmony in Kalaḅarị-Ịjọ. *Issues in African Language and Linguistics*, eds. E. N. Emenanjọ & O-m. Ndimele, 70-81. Aba: Institute of Nigerian Languages.

Akinlabi, A. 1997. Kalaḅarị Vowel Harmony. *The Linguistic Review* 14:97-138.

Akobo, N. T. 1953. *Wa Nimi N'iḅi Aị*. London: James Townsend and Sons.

Black, C. A. 1995. Boundary Tones on Word-internal Domains in Kinande. *Phonology* 12:1-38.

Ḅẹrẹpiki, C. I. 1971. *Kalaḅarị Tarị Go Ḍiri*. Ibadan & Port Harcourt: Rivers Readers Project.

Chomsky, N. 1965. *Aspects of the Theory of Syntax*. Cambridge, Mass.: MIT.

Clark, M. 1992. Representation of Downstep in Dschang Bamileke. *The Phonology of Tone: The Representation of Tonal Register*, eds. H. van der Hulst & K. Snider, 29-74. Berlin: Mouton and Gruyter.

Clarke, J. 1848. *Specimens of Dialects*. Berwick-upon-Tweed: Daniel Cameron.

Claudi, U. & Heine, B. 1989. On the Nominal Morphology of 'Alienability' in some African Languages. *Current Approaches to African Linguistics*, eds. P. Newman & R. D. Botne, 5, 8:3-19.

Clements, G. N. & K. Ford. 1979. Kikuyu Tone Shift and Its Synchronic Consequences. *Linguistic Inquiry* 10:179-210.

Cowper, E. & K. Rice. 1985. The Destruction of Tonal Structure in Mende. *Studies in African Linguistics*, ed. R. Schuh, Supplement 9:57-62.

Dateme, P. T. 1985. Contrastive Analysis of the Phonology of Kalaḅarị and Kiswahili. B.A. Long essay, University of Port Harcourt.

Dike, K. O. 1956. *Trade and Politics in the Niger-Delta*: 1830-1885. Oxford: Clarendon Press.

Elugbe, B. O. 1989. Edoid. *The Niger-Congo Languages*, ed. J. Bendor-Samuel, 291-304. Lanham: University of America Press.

Goldsmith, J. 1976. Autosegmental Phonology. Doctoral dissertation, MIT. Published by Garland Press, New York.

Goldsmith, J. 1990. *Autosegmental and Metrical Phonology*. Oxford: Blackwell.

Haegeman, L. 1997. Introduction: On the Interaction of Theory and Description in Syntax. *The New Comparative Syntax*, ed. L. Haegeman, 1-32. London: Longman.

Halle, M. & G. N. Clements. 1983. *Problem Book in Phonology*. Cambridge, Mass.: MIT.

Haraguchi, S. 1984. Some Tonal and Segmental Effects of Vowel Height in Japanese. *Language and Structure*, ed. M. Aronoff & R. Oehrle, 145-56. Cambridge, Mass.: MIT.

Harry, B. A. 1949. *Kalaḅarị Tarị Go Ḍiri*. Buguma: Bessy Wokoma and Sons Printing Press.

Harry, O. G. (In Progress). Emerging Dialects of Kalaḅarị.

Harry, O.G. 1987. A Phonology of Nkọrọọ. B.A. Long essay, University of Port Harcourt.

Harry, O. G. 1989. A Comparative Reconstruction of Proto-KOIN Phonology. M.A. thesis, University of Port Harcourt.

Harry, O. G. 1995. Pronouns in Language Classification: A Case Study of East Ịjọ. *Issues In African Language and Linguistics*, eds. E. N. Emenanjọ & O-m. Ndimele, 152-61. Aba: Institute of Nigerian Languages.

Harry, O. G. 2003. Illustration of the IPA in Kalaḅarị-Ịjọ. *Journal of the International Phonetic Association* 33.1: 113-120

Hayes, B. 1989. Compensatory Lengthening in Moraic Phonology. *Linguistic Inquiry* 20:253-306.

Hyman, L. 1985a. *A Theory of Phonological Weight*. Dordrecht: Foris.

Hyman, L. 1985b. Word Domains and Downstep in Bamileke-Dschang. *Phonology Yearbook* 2:47-83.

Ibim, O. 1983. The Phonology of Bille. B.A. Long essay, University of Port Harcourt.

Inkelas, S. & D. Zec. 1995. Syntax-Phonology Interface. *The Handbook of Phonological Theory*, ed. J. Goldsmith, 535-49. Oxford: Blackwell.

Iyalla, P.K. 1984. A Comparative Analysis of the Suprasegmentals in Ḅụmọ and Kalaḅarị. B.A. Long essay, University of Port Harcourt.

Jenewari, C. E. W. 1972. *Teachers' Notes on Kalaḅarị Tarị Go Ḍiri*. Ibadan & Port Harcourt: Rivers Readers Project.

Jenewari, C. E. W. 1974. *Kalaḅarị Orthography*. Ibadan & Port Harcourt: Rivers Readers Project. 2nd ed. 1978.

Jenewari, C. E. W. 1977. Studies in Kalaḅarị Syntax. Doctoral dissertation, University of Ibadan.

Jenewari, C. E. W. 1980. A Linguistic Guide to Spoken Kalaḅarị. University of Port Harcourt, Ms.

Jenewari, C. E. W. 1983. *Dẹfaka: Ịjọ's Closest Linguistic Relative*. Port Harcourt: University of Port Harcourt Press.

Jenewari, C. E. W. 1984. The Kalaḅarị Language and Its Present Status. Port Harcourt, Ms.

Jenewari, C. E. W. 1989. Ijoid. *The Niger-Congo Languages*, ed. J. Bendor-Samuel, Lanham: University Press of America.

Jones, G. I. 1963. *The Trading States of the Oil Rivers*. London: Oxford University Press.

Kaisse, E. 1985. *Connected Speech: The Interaction of Syntax and Phonology*. Orlando, FL.: Academic Press.

Kenstowicz, M. 1994. *Phonology in Generative Grammar*. Oxford: Blackwell.

Kiparsky, P. 1982. Lexical Phonology and Morphology. *Linguistics in the Morning Calm*, ed. I. S. Yang, 3-91. Seoul: Hanshin.

Kiparsky, P. 1985. Some Consequences of Lexical Phonology. *Phonology Yearbook* 2:83-138.

Kouwenberg, S. 1993. *A Grammar of Berbice Dutch Creole*. Berlin: Mouton de Gruyter.

Kouwenberg, S. 1996. Grammaticalization and Word Order in the History of Berbice Dutch Creole. *Changing Meanings, Changing Functions. Grammaticalization in Contact Languages*, ed. P. Baker & A. Syea, 207-18. London: University of Westminster Press.

Ladefoged, P. & I. Maddieson. 1996. *The Sounds of the World's Languages*. Oxford: Blackwell.

Ladefoged, P. 1964. *A Phonetic Study of West African languages*. Cambridge: Cambridge University Press.

Leben, W. 1978. The Representation of Tone. *Tone: A Linguistic Survey*, ed. V. Fromkin, 177-219. New York: Academic Press.

Leben, W. 1973, 1980. Suprasegmental Phonology. Doctoral Dissertation, MIT. Published by Garland Pub. Inc.

Lee, J. D. & K. Williamson. 1990. A Lexicostatistic Classification of Ịjọ Dialects. *Research in African Language and Linguistics* 1:1-10.

Lieber, R. 1987. *An Integrated Theory of Autosegmental Processes*. New York: State University of New York Press.

Lindau, M. 1978. Vowel Features. *Language* 54:541-63.

Mohanan, K. P. 1986. *Lexical Phonology*. Dordrecht: Reidel.

Newman, P. Tone and Affixation in Hausa. *Studies in African Linguistics* 17:249-67.

Odden, D. 1987. Kimatuumbi Phrasal Phonology. *Phonology Yearbook* 4:13-26.

Odden, D. 1990. Syntax, Lexical Rules and Postlexical Rules in Kimatuumbi. *The Phonology-Syntax Connection*, eds. S. Inkelas & D. Zec. 259-78. Chicago: University of Chicago Press.

Odden, D. 1995a. Phonology at the Phrasal Level in Bantu. *Bantu Phonology and Morphology*. Lincom Europa Studies in African Linguistics 6, ed. F. Katamba, 40-68. Munchen: Lincom Europa.

Odden, D. 1995b. Tone in African Languages. *The Handbook of Phonological Theory*, ed. J. Goldsmith, 444-475. Oxford: Blackwell.

Odden, D. 1996. *The Phonology and Morphology of Kimatuumbi*. Oxford: Clarendon Press.

Owuye, S. et. al. n.d. Kalaḅarị Dictionary. University of Ibadan & University of Port Harcourt. Ms.

Pulleyblank, D. 1986. *Tone in Lexical Phonology*. Dordrecht: Reidel.

Rocca, I. 1994. *Generative Phonology*. London: Routledge.

Sebba, M. 1987. *The Syntax of Serial Verbs*. Amsterdam: John Benjamins.

Selkirk, E. 1986. On the Derived Domains in Sentence Phonology. *Phonology Yearbook* 3:371-405.

Selkirk, E. & T. Shen. 1990. Prosodic Domains in Shanghai Chinese. *The Phonology-Syntax Connection*, eds. Inkelas, S. & D. Zec, 313-337. Chicago: The University of Chicago Press.

Smith, N. et. al. 1987. The Ịjọ Elements in Berbice Dutch. *Language and Society* 16:49-90.

Stewart, J. M. 1992. Dschang and Ebrié as Akan-type Total Downstep Languages. *The Phonology of Tone: The Representation of Tonal Register*, eds. H. van der Hulst & K. Snider, 185-244. Berlin: Mouton and Gruyter.

Thomas, N. M. 1914. *Specimens of Languages from Southern Nigeria*. London: Harrison and Sons.

Warịḅọkọ, W. 1991. New Calabar and Forces of Change; ca. 1845-1950. Doctoral dissertation, University of Birmingham.

Warịḅọkọ, W. 1998. *Planting Church Culture at New Calabar: Some Neglected Aspects of Missionary Enterprise in the Eastern Delta; ca 1963-1918*. Bethesda: International Scholars Publication.

Welmers, W. E. 1973. *African Language Structures*. Berkeley, Calif.: University of California Press.

Williamson, K. 1969. Ịjọ: *Twelve Nigerian Languages*, ed. E. Dunstan, 49-52. London: Longmans.

Williamson, K. 1972. *Reading and Writing Kalaḅarị*. Ibadan & Port Harcourt: Rivers Readers Project.

Williamson, K. 1988. Tone and Accent in Ịjọ. *Autosegmental Studies in Pitch Accent*, eds. H. van der Hulst & N. Smith, 253-78. Dordrecht: Foris.

Williamson, K. 1989. Niger-Congo Overview. *The Niger-Congo Languages*, ed. J. Bendor-Samuel, Lanham: University Press of America.

Williamson, K. & R. Blench. 2000. Niger-Congo. *African Languages: An Introduction*, eds. B. Heine & D. Nurse, 11-42. Cambridge: Cambridge University Press.

Wolff, H. 1959. Subsystem typologies and Area Linguistics. *Anthropological Linguistics* 7:1-88.

Yip, M. 1988. Template Morphology and the Direction of Association. *Natural Language & Linguistic Theory* 6:551-77.

Zubizarreta, M. L. 1982. The formal Interaction of Harmony and Accent: The Tone Pattern of Japanese. *The Structure of Phonological Representations (Part II)*, eds. Hulst van der H. & N. Smith. 159-212. Dordrecht: Foris Publication.